APPLESEEDS:
A Boy Named Johnny Chapman

Melissa M. Cybulski

Illustrated by T. Lak

Appleseeds: A Boy Named Johnny Chapman
by Melissa M. Cybulski
appleseedsthebook.com

All rights reserved. This book and any portion thereof may not be reproduced or used in any manner whatsoever without the expressed written permission of the author, except for the use of brief quotations in a book review.

Book design, cover and inside illustrations by T.Lak

For Mark, Millie, and Ben

***

For the real-life Nicholas, who never had a last name, but whose voice called out to me before all others as I sat to write this book

***

For all the children like Johnny, who are smart in all sorts of ways
that just aren't measured at school.

To make a prairie it takes a clover and one bee,
One clover, and a bee.
And revery.
The revery alone will do,
If bees are few.

- Emily Dickinson

Contents

Map of Longmeadow 1783	6
Prologue	9
A Delivery	11
Captain Chapman's Orders	23
The Town Green	31
Meeting Nicholas	38
Meeting Eda (and Hitty)	47
Trouble in the Orchard	55
Putting Pen to Paper	65
Nathaniel's Jam	71
The School Teacher	79
First Day	91
School Days	105
Lightning Strikes	119
Incorporation Day	127
School's Out	141
Author's Note	149
Acknowledgments	154

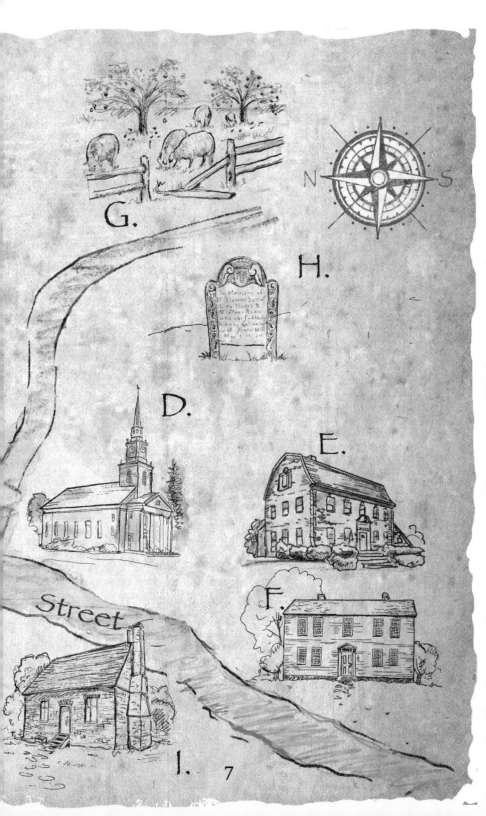

Johnny Chapman's house

Prologue

Once there was a boy named Johnny living in a small town in New England during the last days of the American Revolution. Johnny didn't know it yet, in fact nobody did, but he would grow up to be a legend. That's how famous his name would become. He wasn't going to be a president or an actor. Not a sword fighter or a dragon slayer. But he would become the man who planted the trees that people needed to make them feel at home in a new place.

That is who this story is about: the boy who would become the man who would become the legend. Before he was famous as Johnny Appleseed, he was just a boy – a boy named Johnny Chapman.

He did not grow up wanting to be a legend or hoping to be a legend. He was just an ordinary boy who was happy being just an ordinary boy. All he wanted was good food, sunshine to warm his face, rain to wash the air clean, and his family and good friends to spend his days with.

Johnny was a friend of all the animals, and he knew their different tracks near his Connecticut River Valley home. The beaver tracks down in the meadows were different from the raccoon and skunk tracks around his house. The roaming deer and wild turkey left their marks wherever they wandered, too. Johnny knew them all. He also knew the different trills of the birds: the cardinals, blue jays, and bobolinks among them. He didn't even mind the crows that pestered all the farmers. The cows, the horses, the pigs, the cats, the dogs—all of them were his friends the summer he started school in this new place where he'd come to live.

Eight years old can be a wonderful time. And Johnny Chapman was eight years old in 1783 in Longmeadow, Massachusetts.

That's where our story begins.

A Delivery

"Johnny! Johnny Chapman, where are you?" The call startled Johnny from his hiding place in the elm tree that late spring morning. "Johnny! It's time to get the buckets!"

"On my way!" he replied, as he scurried down the thick branches before landing with a thud on the ground below.

Running barefoot around the back of his house, Johnny Chapman bumped straight into his stepmother. She carried a big bundle of sheets in her arms to throw in the kettle for washing. Monday was laundry day, and that meant Johnny would spend his morning making many trips to Cooley Brook.

"There you are, Johnny," Mother Lucy said.

"There you are, Johnny," his little brother, Nathaniel, echoed.

"Here I am," he said, scooping Nathaniel up into his arms and swinging him around in a circle.

Johnny had two important jobs on Mondays: fetching buckets and buckets and buckets of water for Mother Lucy to wash and rinse the week's dirty clothes and linens and doing his best to keep two-year-old Nathaniel out of trouble.

It was early May. The grass felt wet and cool under his bare feet. The sun already had the tinge of warmth that let him know that spring was nearly over and summer would soon be full upon them.

Time to get the buckets

Fetching water from the brook was usually one of Johnny's favorite chores. It wasn't as easy as getting it from the well in the kitchen yard, but the well was running low and they needed it for drinking until his father could dig a new one. Getting water from Cooley Brook gave Johnny a chance to do what he loved best—walk in the woods near his house. As long as he brought home the water in a timely manner, how he spent his time to and from the brook was up to him. He wasn't allowed to bring little Nathaniel with him. Mother Lucy feared that little children couldn't help but get too close to the water.

On his first trip to Cooley Brook, Johnny imagined himself a light-limbed squirrel jumping from branch to branch, sometimes pausing to listen to the sounds of twittering birds and the breeze through the bright green leaves. On his way back, weighed down with a heavy wooden bucket filled with fresh water, he imagined himself more like a new colt on wobbly legs.

By his third trip to the brook, his arms ached and his back stiffened as he lugged the heavy wooden bucket, trying not to spill too much water. Mother Lucy promised him a thick slice of last night's potato-apple pie to reward him and build him up for the next few trips back and forth. That certainly helped as he lugged back his third and sloshiest bucket.

"Thank you, Johnny," Mother Lucy said as she placed the new baby in the cradle she had brought outside. She liked to have him nearby in case he fussed. "Now come sit with me and Nathaniel while baby Abner is quiet. Have a bit of this nice pie from yesterday's supper."

Johnny gladly took a seat on the bench at the work table. "Yes, please! I love potato-apple pie."

Mother Lucy cut him a big piece. "I am so grateful for the apple tree my uncle planted here so many years ago," she said. "We may not have much, but we do have that tree to provide fine fruit for us. And what we don't need now we can preserve to last us through the winter. See the pink flowers? The tree is already blossoming again. Before you know it, a new harvest of apples will follow. Even the smallest of homes can find space for a tree as useful as this one."

Johnny's home was indeed small—and nearly one hundred years old when his father and stepmother, Mother Lucy, got married and moved into it. Johnny was six years old and living with his grandparents in Leominster at the time, waiting for the war to be over. Captain Chapman told Johnny that General George Washington needed him to fight for freedom from ol' King George's tyranny.

Johnny didn't know what tyranny was. He just knew that his father had to be away at war and that his mother had died from a terrible cough. Coming to live in Longmeadow felt strange and new to Johnny at first, especially since his older sister, Elizabeth, stayed behind with his grandparents. But Mother Lucy was kind, and she made Johnny feel at home right away.

Sitting on the bench and letting his arms rest was a relief after lugging those heavy buckets filled with water. One by one, Mother Lucy poured them into the big, steaming kettle over the fire in the yard outside their front door. The smoky smell of wood and ash filled the air. Nathaniel climbed eagerly onto Johnny's lap and clapped his hands in glee as his big brother made his favorite silly faces at him.

Johnny knew how to make Nathaniel giggle and laugh better than anyone else. He was proud of that. He sat on the edge of the bench that held the washtubs, Nathaniel on his lap and a piece of potato-apple pie in his hands. He wanted to eat it slowly and carefully to savor every crumb, but his little brother would think it funnier if he pretended to snuffle and eat it greedily like the pigs. So Johnny did a little of both, savoring and snuffling while Mother Lucy gently rocked Baby Abner's cradle with her foot and smiled at the boys' antics.

"Washing day is the hardest day, Johnny, so I am glad to have your help and company for your brothers and me."

"Oh, I don't mind," said Johnny, "especially now that the winter has passed and the woods are waking up."

He scanned the sky and continued. "I like

to keep a checklist in my mind of all the things I see and the sounds I hear for every season. For spring: rabbits. Check. Dandelions. Check. Rabbits nibbling dandelions. Check. Twittering birds. Check, check, and check. Do you ever wonder what they say to each other?"

"Can't say I ever really thought about it, Johnny," replied Mother Lucy. "Have you any idea what they are saying?"

Johnny answered in his best high-pitched, twittering bird voice that instantly captured Nathaniel's attention. "Tweet, tweet! Sunny skies! Tweet, tweet! Last night's rain brought up good, fat worms! Tweet, tweet! Time to build a new nest! Too many hawks around!"

"Ha, ha! Perhaps that's true!" Mother Lucy laughed. "It's nice to hear their songs first thing in the morning. It makes for a pleasant start to the day. You never do hear a grumpy bird, do you?"

In his cradle, Baby Abner stretched. He searched for his fist to suck on from under his blanket.

"Speaking of grumpy birds," Mother Lucy

said, "Baby Abner will wake any minute grumpy to be fed. It's best to keep working and not let any more of this day get away from us. I think a few more buckets of fresh water for rinsing will be all that's left. Alright, Nathaniel, let your big brother get back to work."

Nathaniel pouted, but Johnny tickled his tummy and tweet-tweeted in his ear as he slid him off his lap.

"Don't worry, I'll be back in no time, and I'll bring you a special treasure from the woods." Johnny picked up the rope handle of the bucket, his hand red and raw from his previous trips, and off he went thinking about bird songs and potato-apple pie.

A little way past his house, a horse approached. Colonel Jonathan Hale, who lived on the town green, drew near. He earned his rank in the war with Great Britain, just as Johnny's father had. Colonel Hale answered the first call to arms at Lexington in April 1775. When Johnny saw him approaching on his large, black horse, he stepped aside to make room for him.

Johnny was surprised when Colonel Hale

slowed his horse and tipped his hat.

"You are Captain Chapman's boy, aren't you?"

"Yes, sir," Johnny answered hesitantly, shading his eyes from the sun as he looked up at Colonel Hale. Something about the beautiful and powerful black horse and the striking scene of Colonel Hale astride it made Johnny feel small and shy.

"Well, then, I am very happy to meet you here. Would you mind helping me complete a mission this morning?"

"No, sir, I wouldn't mind," Johnny replied, wondering what it might be.

"Perfect. I need you to be my messenger." Colonel Hale reached into his saddlebag. "Your father asked that I set these items aside for him in my store. I figured I'd save him the trip to the green and drop them off on my way to Springfield." He handed Johnny a pint bottle of a dark-colored liquid that Johnny recognized from his kitchen as rum, and some sugar, packed tightly in paper tied with a string. "That may be heavy, but you look strong enough to handle it."

"Yes, sir," said Johnny, placing the items into the empty bucket he was carrying.

"Now bring that straight home and tell your father he may settle with me at the store when he is able. I hear there is a new baby in the Chapman house. Another boy?"

"Yes, sir," said Johnny, "named Abner. After Mother Lucy's brother."

"Ah, yes, Abner Cooley. I remember him well. Sadly gone too soon, just like his father before him. Well, a lucky man your father is to have healthy children. Be sure to tell him that school will soon start for the summer session at the brick schoolhouse. I hope you will be among the students this term."

Johnny instantly felt a flutter in his stomach as the colonel said this.

He continued. "We've got a fine young schoolmistress coming to us from Enfield. Now that the war is over, Massachusetts needs bright, helpful young children like you to continue the work we started. Stop by the store anytime. There is nothing Mrs. Hale likes more than sneaking gingerbread to the great young minds of Longmeadow. Good day to you, Johnny Chapman."

"Yes, sir. Good day, sir."

Colonel Hale and his majestic black horse continued down the road toward Springfield. Johnny turned toward home to drop off the delivery as an uncomfortable feeling crept into his bones.

Colonel Hale had just mentioned one of Johnny's least favorite words: school. Last term did not go so well for Johnny.

Cooley Brook

Captain Chapman's Orders

That evening during a supper of baked beans, fresh fish, and the last of the potato-apple pie, Johnny's father shared the news of his day. He found work building Reverend Storrs' new house. Because the Chapmans did not own a large farm like some of the other families in Longmeadow, Captain Chapman had to rely on his hands and skills in other ways to earn money.

The war was over now, which was good, but that meant his father no longer had a job. Johnny's father had been stationed at the Springfield Arsenal for three years, leading a regiment of men repairing damaged cannon and carriage wheels from the battlefields. There was no need for that kind of work anymore, particularly in Western Massachusetts. But for the time being, the family could count on the work of building Reverend Storrs' house, and that was a good thing. When the work was gone, the money would be gone until he found his next job.

Johnny felt nervous inside knowing he had news to share after supper. School was a topic that filled Johnny with worry. In 1783, school was in session two times a year: in the winter and in the summer. Last term, the teacher, Master Simeon Loomis, embarrassed him several times because he was having a hard time reading aloud. But Johnny couldn't disobey Colonel Hale's request.

Potato apple pie

Nervously, Johnny began, "Colonel Hale came by today, Father, to drop off some rum and sugar from the store."

"Did he?" asked his father. "That was good of him. Did he bring any news from his end of the green?"

"Not really, sir," Johnny answered, half wondering if he should mention the dreaded "S" word after all. But he knew that his father would find out sooner or later that a new school term would be starting. He figured it might be better if he heard it at home where Johnny could remind him about the trouble they had with the old schoolmaster.

"Actually," Johnny continued slowly, "he mentioned that the summer term for school will be starting soon, and he was wondering if I was going to be there."

"Oh, I see," said Captain Chapman, taking a scoop of baked beans and chewing thoughtfully before responding. "Did he mention who the schoolmaster would be?"

"No, sir, not by name. But he did say it would be a schoolmistress this time. From Enfield."

"I sure hope that she will be better than the one they hired last term," added Mother Lucy as she cradled Abner in one arm and encouraged Nathaniel to eat with the other.

Johnny cringed. He was not what anyone would call a "strong student" and after a few weeks, had begged not to go back to face Master Loomis. Johnny was the kind of boy who was naturally smart about a whole lot of things that just didn't seem to matter at school. He could identify birds by their calls and trees by their leaves. He had a natural kindness and softness to his fellow creatures, both animal and human, that just couldn't be taught at school.

Unfortunately for Johnny, Master Loomis cared more about sitting perfectly still in a seat, reading aloud from the spelling book, and reciting memorized verses. Those were all difficult for Johnny. The schoolmaster called Johnny a "halfwit" and yelled at him to sit straight and keep his eyes and ears open so some learning might seep into his head. Master Loomis even said he was scared for the fate of the new nation if "addle-brained children like

Johnny Chapman" were its future.

That was too much for Captain Chapman. He marched straight over to the school—with Johnny hurrying to keep up—to give Master Loomis a piece of his mind after Johnny came home in tears during the noon recess.

"Dreamers like Johnny are exactly what this new nation needs," he said firmly to Master Loomis. Master Loomis stood quietly, too stunned to speak. Johnny was glad his classmates were still playing outside.

"This country was built on ideas and dreams," Captain Chapman said. "And as long as an uninspired teacher like you is leading this classroom, my son will be doing his learning at home."

And that was the end of the school term for Johnny. He was happy to have his father's confidence in him. It helped, but it didn't take away the shame Master Loomis made him feel. That was the power of words. Once they were spoken, there was no taking them back. And some words were hurtful.

Perhaps that was why Johnny was so

careful with his words. He knew what it was to be stung by them. The idea of a new school term made him feel scared and uneasy all over again.

"Father, would I be able to continue learning at home this term?" he asked hopefully.

Captain Chapman looked across the table at his wife. "Well," he began slowly, "I don't think that would be a good idea this time around."

Johnny's heart sank.

His father continued. "With little Nate underfoot and a new baby on top of that, plus all the work that needs to be done during the day, I imagine your stepmother doesn't have the time to help you with your schooling right now. And besides, just because you had one bad experience with one bad teacher doesn't mean you give up. What if General Washington gave up after the first battle that didn't go his way? Why, we'd still be under the thumb of King George!"

"But, I could be a real help here with the chores and with the little ones," Johnny tried.

"And I could practice my writing and reading in the meantime. You'd like that, Mother Lucy, wouldn't you?" he asked hopefully, turning to a potential ally.

"Oh, yes, Johnny, you certainly are a big help around here, especially with your brothers," she said gently. "But it's time for you to do something for yourself now. You've mastered your letters, but when it comes to reading and writing and arithmetic, you need more than I am able to give to you right now. I never learned to read and write properly myself. I do wish I had."

"And," Captain Chapman continued, "I heard some talk at Reverend Storrs' house that the town just ordered a set of new schoolbooks fresh off the presses. By a Hartford man. Webster, I think his name is. Got people all over the area excited." Johnny's father added, "We can't give you that here. There's no extra money for books, but at school you can have one. It's the first real American schoolbook. That's quite an opportunity for you, Johnny."

Mother Lucy added, "And my mother tells me that the new teacher will be living with Colonel and Mrs. Hale this term. Her family lives too far away for her to make it to and from the schoolhouse every day. She's a young lady about my age, Johnny! I'm sure you'll do really well with her. I just know she will see your gifts right away—just as I did when we met."

"So that's settled then," said Captain Chapman. "Why don't we finish up supper here and take a walk down to the river before it gets too dark? We can see if anything interesting came in at the dock. Tomorrow, you can bring a note to Colonel Hale arranging payment for my bill at the store. See what you can find out about when school will start."

Johnny sat quietly, knowing that the decision had already been made. He knew better than to question his father's orders. Those would be wasted words. He was going to school, like it or not.

The Town Green

The next morning, after Johnny made his bed, hauled up some water, brought in wood shavings for the fire, and played with his younger brothers, Mother Lucy gave him the note his father had written to bring to Colonel Hale.

Johnny set off on the one-mile walk toward the Longmeadow green, the grassy area surrounded by the meetinghouse, shops, a tavern, a schoolhouse, and several homes. The town green was always a busy place. Children from the houses around it often played outside, kicking up dust as they chased each other along the dirt road. Men in waistcoats and breeches talked about important matters. Ladies in long, apron-covered dresses with kerchiefs tied around their necks carried baskets to and from neighborly visits, also talking about important matters. Horses carrying riders on errands from Springfield and Northampton were tied at posts outside the wooden homes and businesses.

Mother Lucy always expected Johnny to take a little extra care in his appearance when he was heading over to the green. She helped him wash the dirt from his sun-tanned face and hands. She tried to tame his dark hair—which always seemed to stick up in different directions—and instructed him to tuck his shirt into his breeches, and at least carry his shoes with him so he could put them on when he arrived. Johnny rarely wore shoes. They pinched his toes and made his feet feel all stuffy.

Walking the short distance to the main road, Johnny went on his errand. Like fetching water, his time was his own on the walk. He could have all the thinkings and imaginings he wanted. Today, the weather was sunny and warm, and he tucked the note for Colonel Hale into the shoes he carried. That way he had a free hand to collect rocks that had the perfect amount of special, whether it was their smoothness, color, or shape. The shoes he carried were the perfect place to hold the rocks he collected. By the time Johnny got to the green, one shoe was heavy with perfect stones.

He traveled past the dingle and Wheel Meadow Brook, resisting the temptation to leave the road for a little exploring. He passed Mr. Ely's fine brick house on his right and the site where Reverend Storrs' new house was being built on his left. The frame was standing, and stacks of freshly cut pine boards waited to be put in place. Johnny looked for his father among the builders but didn't see him.

Whenever Johnny approached the green, one of the first things he did was to look for the rooster—a bright golden weathervane sitting atop the meetinghouse steeple. He liked to guess which direction the rooster would be facing based on which way the wind blew. He was usually correct because he paid attention to the breeze as he walked. The rooster always faced the direction the wind was coming from. You could say the rooster looked as proud as a peacock… but he wasn't a peacock of course. As regal as a rooster, maybe? But "regal" was a word for kings, and there were no more kings in America. Johnny would have to keep think-

Meetinghouse Rooster

ing about a word to describe the rooster.

The meetinghouse he passed was a long, rectangular building painted white. It was used for church and town meetings. Inside its tall steeple hung an enormous bell. This year, Lieutenant Festus Colton was in charge of ringing the bell to call people from their homes and farms whenever there was news to share. Before there was a bell in the steeple, a man was paid to walk through the streets banging a drum to let people know it was time to gather. The clanging of the bell certainly carried farther than the drum. Johnny could hear it a mile away at his home.

Today, there was no bell ringing as Johnny passed the tavern at the red house, where travelers could spend the night after a good meal and some fine conversation. Some of the Coltons lived there. Poor Mrs. Colton sure had her hands full with running the tavern and caring for several little children all around Johnny's age.

Next, he paused to look at the brick schoolhouse on the green. He remembered the crack and the sting of Master Loomis' ruler on his hand, punishing him for staring out the window.

    The terrible memory was thankfully interrupted by a butterfly swooping down in front of his face from out of nowhere. Actually, there were two butterflies twirling and chasing each other in a playful, tumbling pattern. Johnny followed them, ducking and bobbing as they did, right up to the front of Colonel Hale's house and store.

    Colonel Hale's shop wasn't the only store in town, but it sold items that farmers' families needed at fair prices. In a simple wooden room he built onto the side of his house, you could find supplies like sugar, nails, and brooms on shelves. If you had bushels of onions to spare, or extra butter, or a cider press to turn a harvest of apples into barrels of cider, you could trade with Colonel Hale for items you needed. He would rent out his horses if you needed to travel, his sleigh if you needed to travel in winter, and at this time of year, his enormous soap kettle so families could make their yearly supply of soap. Money was rarely exchanged at Colonel Hale's store, which was exactly why

Captain Chapman liked to do his business there. Johnny's father didn't often have money to spend, but he was skilled with his hands and willing to work. He used that to barter for supplies for his family.

Johnny didn't often get to go to the green alone, so he was feeling very grown-up. The rooster weathervane faced west as he sat on the red sandstone steps to dump out the rocks he'd stored in his shoe. He took the note from the other one and slipped the shoes onto his feet. He hoped to complete his errand quickly and then head down into that dingle by Wheel Meadow Brook to hunt for raspberries before going home.

Little did he know he'd leave Colonel Hale's shop with much more important plans.

Meeting Nicholas

Johnny pushed on the wooden door's latch and entered the quiet, cool, dark space inside the store. As his eyes adjusted to the change in light, he was surprised to see that the only other person in the store was a boy, like him. He sat behind the counter, spectacles on his face, reading a newspaper spread out before him. The boy was so absorbed by his reading that he didn't look up when Johnny entered. Johnny stood for several seconds at the door before the boy, whose name was Nicholas, sensed his presence and looked up.

"Good day," said Nicholas.

"Good day," Johnny replied.

"Can I help you with something?" asked Nicholas, standing up.

Johnny didn't know what to make of the scene. He recognized the boy, a Black boy, with dark skin and close-cropped hair, because they both sat in the balcony at church services on Sunday, but they had never spoken to each other. Johnny had been expecting to see an adult like Colonel Hale or his wife working at the store—not a child his own age.

"Oh, um, I was looking for Colonel Hale to give him this note," said Johnny when he found his voice. "Or Mrs. Hale maybe?"

"Is this in reference to the store?" asked Nicholas formally.

"Um, yes," replied Johnny, holding up his father's note. "From my father. About paying for a delivery."

"Ah, I can take that for you then," said Nicholas, carefully folding his newspaper and reaching for a thick, well-worn, ledger book. "I will make a note here for Colonel Hale when he returns. And what is your father's name?"

"Captain Chapman," replied Johnny, stepping forward to give the paper to this extraordinary boy. As he handed him the note, Johnny realized that the boy's spectacles actually had no glass in them. They were just frames! He watched Nicholas carefully read the note, then flipped through the ledger book to find Captain Chapman's account page. He dipped a quill pen into an ink pot and copied the note's message in the proper place.

Johnny all of a sudden had a lot of questions.

He started with, "Excuse me, what's your name?"

"Nicholas," came the reply.

"Why are you sitting back there?" was Johnny's next question.

"Because I am free to."

Johnny carefully followed up with, "I mean, do you work here? You just seem young to be behind the counter reading the newspaper and keeping the record books."

"Yes, I work here, and I live here with Phillis. We have a room. Our own room. Phillis sews for the store. Colonel Hale pays her a good price for her work. And he pays me, too, for keeping my eye on the store when he and Mrs. Hale are busy."

"Who is Phillis?"

"She's like my mother, I guess."

"Oh," Johnny replied. He had more questions, but as a boy whose own mother had died, he knew better than to ask too many questions about where someone's mother might be.

"How'd you learn to read and write like that?" Johnny asked.

"I don't know exactly. Just feels like something I could always do. Phillis helped me at first. We used to live at Reverend Williams' house. When he was alive, he had a whole room of books, and I would just sit and look through those books if I wasn't in the way and wasn't needed for work."

"Did you work for Reverend Williams?" Johnny asked.

"Not for money or anything. We had to. He enslaved us. But he died last year. Since the war, no one can be enslaved in Massachusetts anymore, and we are free people. Now Phillis and I can choose where we want to live and work, and we choose here."

Nicholas looked around the shelves. "Colonel Hale doesn't have half as many books as Reverend Williams did, but the ones he does have are much more interesting. And he gets the newspapers from Hartford and Boston, and the new one from Springfield. Those are almost better than the books because there are stories of things like shipwrecks and robberies. Reverend Williams mostly had books about church and prayer. Nothing very interesting ever happened."

"I'm not very good at reading anything," said Johnny. "It just never seems to make sense. The words just blur together or move all over the page. And I'm definitely no good at all with a quill pen. I've tried to use ink, but I just make a mess. I end up with lots of ink blots and smudges."

"I used to do that, too," said Nicholas, "but I learned how to keep my hand steady, my quill sharpened, and my ink nice and light. Here, watch." He took a clean piece of scrap paper from a drawer and placed it on the counter. Carefully, he inspected the tip of the white quill pen he just used, dipped it ever so gently into the inkstand, and wiped off the extra ink against the rim. He placed one hand against the top of the paper to hold it steady, and with the other he carefully wrote out his name.

Nicholas Peters

"See? I've been practicing for someday when someone needs me to sign a contract or deed. I like the sound of the quill scratching on the paper as I go. I could just write and write and write and write to hear that sound. I don't have much reason to do that now, I suppose. But hopefully someday."

"That's really good," said Johnny. "And that's your whole name?"

"Yes, Nicholas Peters. Phillis thought that would be a good last name for us since we didn't have one before. At Reverend Williams' house, she was always just Phillis and I was always just Nicholas. But when we got our freedom, she said it was time we had our own last name to start our own family. Peter was her husband. He was owned by someone else before he died. They were married for a long time but were never allowed to live together."

"Why not?" asked Johnny.

"Don't know. That's just the way it always was for them. But when we got our freedom, Phillis said, 'My heart was Peter's and Peter's was mine' and that was that. We took the last name Peters."

Johnny was quiet as he stared at Nicholas's handwritten name, thinking about what it meant.

"Can you make my name look like that?" he asked.

"Well, you can try on your own if you'd like," Nicholas said, handing the quill toward Johnny.

"Oh, no, I could never do it like that," said Johnny. "Can you just do it and show me?"

"Well, all right, I guess. But the only way to learn yourself is by practicing. There's no harm in making mistakes in the beginning as you learn something new. Now, what's your name?"

"Johnny. Well, John, actually. John Chapman."

"J-O-H-N?"

"Yes," said Johnny.

"And Chapman, C-H-A-P-M-A-N?"

"Sounds right," said Johnny.

"All right." Right below his own name, Nicholas smoothly wrote it out.

John Chapman

Johnny looked in awe at the swirling letters Nicholas formed.

"That's it?" he asked. "That's me?" He seemed surprised that anything that had to do with him could be so…fancy. Without a second thought, Johnny said, "I want to do that! I want to write like that! Can you teach me how to do that?"

"I suppose," said Nicholas.

Just then, a plump, middle-aged woman dressed in a tidy gown and crisp apron appeared through the door that led into the house.

"Why, hello there, Nicholas," Mrs. Hale said brightly. "I see you have a customer. Now, who do we have here? You do look familiar."

"This is John Chapman, the Captain's boy, ma'am. Come to deliver a note for his father's account."

"Ah, yes. So now I recognize you," she said. "I hear there is a new baby in the family, yes?"

"Yes, ma'am," said Johnny. "Abner."

"Well, then, I'm definitely going to need to send you home with some goodies for your family's table. It's quiet now. How about you two boys follow me into the kitchen? I've got some fresh gingerbread made up from this morning and some cider in the jug. Then I'll see what I've got to send home with you to save your mother some time with the cooking, young Mr. Chapman."

    Johnny and Nicholas exchanged happy glances and followed Mrs. Hale into the kitchen. Gingerbread and cider were always nice.

    But making a new friend was even nicer.

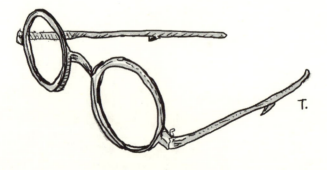

Nicholas' spectacles

Meeting Eda (and Hitty)

A little while later, Johnny left the Hale's shop with a basket of biscuits, marmalade, and some salt pork to bring home as a gift to celebrate the new baby. But Johnny also left with plans to come back in a few days to spend time with Nicholas in the shop and work on his reading, and maybe even his writing. Mrs. Hale had told him all she knew of the new teacher, Miss Polly Reynolds, who would be coming to live with them in a few weeks to teach the summer term of school. Mrs. Hale knew what a good reader Nicholas was, and she thought it would be good for the boys to spend some time with children their own age, learning from each other.

"Johnny, Nicholas can share with you what helped him become a reader and writer, and perhaps you can show him what you like to do outside in the woods around your home. I'm sure Phillis would agree that Nicholas spends far too much time inside. A little sunshine and fresh air will be good for him—both body and soul," she had said.

Johnny knew he had been away from home longer than expected. He quickly kicked off his shoes to free his feet from their burden as he headed back up the green toward home. There would be no time to look for raspberries in the dingle today.

Before he even made it twenty paces, he heard someone call after him. Turning toward the voice, Johnny saw two young girls—one about nine years old and a younger one about five years old, hurrying after him. The older one, red hair blowing in a mass of curls down her back, dragged the smaller one to keep up.

"Good day! Hello there! Good day!" she hollered in Johnny's direction, waving her free hand eagerly. Johnny paused to let her catch up. He didn't respond, though. He didn't really have a chance to as the girl erupted into a stream of conversation that moved too fast for Johnny to follow along.

"Good day, there! Hello! I know you. I remember you! Do you remember me? You are

Johnny Chapman from winter term at school! I recognize you! That schoolmaster was absolutely horrible to you, wasn't he? He was absolutely horrible! I didn't know what happened to you when you stopped coming to school, but then I saw you at church in the meetinghouse and I thought to myself, 'Oh, there he is!' and I was so glad to see that you were there and that Master Loomis hadn't chased you entirely away. I'm supposed to be thinking about my prayers at church, I know, but it's just so awfully long sometimes, isn't it? I can't possibly think solemn thoughts all the time without other thoughts creeping in, can I?"

Again, Johnny could barely begin to open his mouth to respond before the little red-haired girl began again.

"I'm Editha Keep. But you can call me Eda. And this is my sister, Hitty. She's five, but I'm nine. Well, almost. Sylvie, our older sister, is nearly eighteen. Oh, what a bother she is! She's no fun anymore since she got engaged. And Lucy and Sarah Burt next door hardly ever get let out anymore since their brother, Solomon, died in the powder mill explosion.

Did you hear about the powder mill explosion? That was terrible! Mrs. Burt doesn't want to lose any more children. She won't even let them go to school though it's practically right in their front yard. Sometimes I see Lucy and Sarah sitting on their front step in their fine dresses with their needlework on their laps, and I think how terrible that must be to be kept in their house every day. On Sabbath, I sit outside with Hitty and wait for them to walk by with their family. They always have the prettiest bonnets and softest-looking red shoes poking out from under their dresses. And they each carry their own bibles with them like little ladies. I have my own, too, but it's Sylvie's old one. We live right there in the white house

Sylvie's old Bible

next door to Colonel Hale's. The one with the brown door. My family has been in Longmeadow for generations. Just like the Cooleys. Your new mother is a Cooley, right? I'd like to ask what happened to your mama, but I know it's not polite. But you can tell me if you'd like." She waited a beat for Johnny to respond.

"Do you think you want to tell me?"

"I'm sorry, tell you what?" Johnny asked. He was having a hard time keeping up with the pace of the conversation and half of his mind was still back at the powder mill explosion question.

"Your mother? Did she die? Is that why you moved out here when your father married Lucy Cooley? That's what people were saying."

"Oh, that," said Johnny. "Yes, that's what happened. She died when I was two."

"Oh, that's so tragic. That happened to Eleanor Rumrill, too. Then her father married Mary Bliss so she and her brothers would have a mother. They are a very nice family. But there I go again, don't I? Chattering on. Sylvie says I am a chatterbox and need to hold my thoughts and words better. And I try. Don't I try, Hitty? Do you think so? Do you think I'm a chatterbox?" she asked Johnny.

Eda paused long enough for him to say, "Um, I um—"

She picked right back up. "I know I have a habit of going on and on. It's just that I try to hold my tongue, but the words all come tumbling out, and once I've said what I wanted to say I feel better. I'm just ever so curious and I get so excited to see other people, particularly friends. That's the best part of school starting up again soon. A whole summer with friends!" she squealed. "Of course, schoolwork too, but I don't mind that at all because I know at least three times a day we'll be outside with each other at recess. I just love school!"

The whole time Eda chatted on, she and Hitty walked alongside Johnny. He wondered if they would escort him all the way home.

"I do hope you'll come back to school this term, Johnny," she continued. "My father was on the committee to hire the teachers for Longmeadow. He says he got us a fine one. She is absolutely lovely, I hear. Miss Reynolds is her name. Very different from cranky old Master Loomis. Ugh, he was dreadful. He made poor Hitty cry nearly every day, even though she was only one of the babies in the class."

Eda dropped her voice low and did her best impression of Master Loomis' stern voice.

"He would say, 'Mehittable Keep, if you are unable to control those legs of yours from swinging in your seat then you will stand by your seat all day, and if I see you so much as move an inch I will swat your hand with all the inches on my wooden ruler!' I hear he's moved across the river now. I hope they don't ever send him back."

Johnny looked toward Hitty. Her expression changed as she thought of the painful memory.

"Yes, he was mean for sure," said Johnny.

"But you'll come back, won't you? For Miss Reynolds' term? I have ever so many recess games I am ready to play, like huzzlecap (but we can play with pebbles instead of pennies) and blind man's bluff. I'm absolutely terrible at cup and ball, but I really like group games. And the more children, the merrier.

Well, maybe not Margaret Pratt. She can be so mean! She knew how terrible Master Loomis could be last winter and she would still tattle on people. I would just love to tattle on her sometimes, but I bet that she would turn on Hitty rather than me because that's the kind of mean she is. She's t-r-o-u-b-l-e if you know what I mean." Johnny nodded even though he was still trying to arrange the letters he'd just heard into a word that made sense.

"Oh, Hitty! We've come further than we ought to without Mother's permission. She doesn't like it when we go too far past the green. We better turn around here. So nice to see you, Johnny! Say goodbye to Johnny, Hitty. Good day to you and your family!" And back they turned toward the green.

Johnny was left all in a whirl, still carrying the basket of goods from Mrs. Hale, wondering something about a powder mill explosion, and remembering the swirl of letters spelling out his name on Nicholas' paper.

Trouble in the Orchard

The next few weeks were fun for Johnny. After morning chores and playtime with his brothers, Johnny would take his midday meal—packed up in a leather pouch and slung over his shoulder—and head toward the green to meet Nicholas. They would sit outside Colonel Hale's store in the sunshine together, eat their lunches, and talk about the things that mattered to them: what they liked to play, what they didn't like to play, and chores that took up too much of their time.

After eating, the boys would head back into Colonel Hale's store to get to work—the work of helping Johnny learn to read and write. Nicholas was a good teacher. Both boys shared a quiet seriousness and kindness that made them good partners. Nicholas mostly taught by simply sharing the things that were interesting to him. They did not start with schoolbooks but with newspapers instead.

They particularly loved advertisements for missing animals.

"Do you think they ran away on their own or were stolen?" Nicholas sometimes wondered aloud.

"Don't know," Johnny would answer. "Maybe they just wandered away and got lost. But sometimes I see those oxen with the heavy yokes around their necks and I feel uncomfortable just looking at them. Doesn't seem to me that any creature would choose that life if he could."

When the shop was quiet, the boys sat on cider barrels behind the counter with the latest issue of *The Massachusetts Gazette*. Johnny could focus better if they didn't sit in front of the open window because there were just too many distractions outside, with the green leaves of late May blowing on the trees, the bees buzzing around the flowering bushes, and the people walking to and fro on the green as they went about their errands.

Nicholas would begin by blocking off one small section of the newspaper page for Johnny to focus on, asking him what letters he could identify. Johnny was very good at that. Next came small words: *the, and, it, last, from.* Then animal words and colors: *cow, calf, horse, brown, black, white.* Then bigger words: *missing, reward, pasture, taken.* The rest they worked to fill in together by sounding them out and making educated guesses.

By the end of the first couple of weeks, Johnny was able to read:

> Ran away last week from its owner, a small brown horse, with three white Feet. Somewhat lame, -Thin, but high Spirits - trots and paces, - Whoever finds him and will bring said horse to me, or give Information where he may be found, shall receive a reward
>
> Samuel Stebbins
> Longmeadow, May 2, 1783

Looking for missing animals became how they spent part of their time together. Naturally, Eda and Hitty Keep joined them for this detective work. Eda had a keen sense of when the boys were outside and free to run around the green. She always seemed to appear, Hitty trailing behind, and their mother hollering out the window to stay together.

"How should we spend the reward money?" Nicholas wondered.

"I know how I want to spend it!" said Eda. "Candy!"

"I'd like my own books so I don't have to borrow them," said Nicholas.

"I'd like to buy Nathaniel a Noah's Ark with the animals," said Johnny.

"What about you, Hitty?" Eda asked her sister.

"A new dress for my dolly." Hitty quickly answered, as if she'd been thinking about it for a long time.

Though they never did find any of the missing animals from the newspapers, they returned four cats (that were never lost to begin with), two dogs (that also weren't lost but were happy for the attention), six chickens, and one pig to their rightful homes. They were rewarded with amused smiles and thanks from most people, cool drinks, and delicious treats.

The friends were pretty pleased with themselves.

Johnny would return home before sunset to wash up, have supper, play with his brothers, complete some evening chores, and tell his adventures to Mother Lucy and his father, all before heading to bed. In the morning, he'd wake up and do it all over again.

One day, while out searching the green for signs of about a half-dozen of Ebenezer Bliss' sheep that had gone missing from the meadows, the children found themselves in the orchard of Mr. William Forsyth. His orchard was located just across the road from the cemetery behind the meetinghouse. It contained four acres of neatly planted fruit trees. Most were apple, but there were a few pear and peach trees around the border. Mr. Forsyth took the business of his fruit trees very seriously. He spent time every spring out with a brush and a bucket, washing each tree trunk with a mixture of soft soap, lime, and water.

"Why do you wash your fruit tree's trunks with soap?" Johnny asked him one day.

"Aren't they just going to get dirty again being outside?"

"It's not about them getting dirty, Johnny Chapman," Mr. Forsyth told him. "It's about keeping them clean. That wash keeps insect eggs and moss off so my trees can spend all their energy growing good fruit instead of fighting the canker."

While looking for the wandering sheep, Johnny, Nicholas, Eda, and Hitty walked through the cemetery, wondering aloud about

Headstone of Solomon Burt

some of the writing on the headstones. Mother Lucy's father, who had died of smallpox inoculation, was buried here, as well as Solomon Burt, who Eda told them died in a powder mill explosion when he was just nineteen years old. The carving on their headstones told the story of how their lives were lived or how they ended. There were no signs of the missing sheep, though.

Loud yelling from across the road in Mr. Forsyth's orchard made them go running in that direction. They could see right away that some rails in the fence that separated his orchard from the road had been trampled down. Sure enough, on the other side of that fence, stood all six of Mr. Bliss' missing sheep. They were very large, had recently been shorn of their wooly coats in anticipation of summer, and were happily nibbling the bark and low-hanging branches of Mr. Forsyth's apple trees.

"Hey-ah! Get out of here!" Mr. Forsyth hollered. He yelled and waved his arms in big circles, trying to scare the sheep from his trees. They weren't too bothered though. They simply moved from one tree to another, nibbling as quickly as they could.

"Get over here, children!" he yelled in their direction. "Help me get these creatures out of here! They are going to ruin my trees!"

The friends raced over, hollering along and swinging their own arms. They formed a semicircle with Mr. Forsyth to try and corral the sheep into one area. Working together, they gathered the naughty nibblers and coaxed them away from the trees and out of the orchard the same way they came in—through

Sheep in the orchard

the break in the fence. Off the sheep ran, straight down the road east, to look for a new place to cause trouble.

Only then did they notice little Hitty swatting at her hair and screaming. "Bees! Bees!" she cried. "They're stinging me!"

Somewhere in the tall grass, Hitty must have attracted the attention of curious bees. Everyone knew that bees loved the sweet smell of apple blossoms, and Mr. Forsyth's orchard was awash in the pink flowers of the season. It seemed Hitty was pretty sweet to them as well. Eda swatted at them, but it was too late. Poor Hitty managed to get several bee stings, mostly on her neck and hands, as the rest of her was covered by her long dress and the cap on her head.

Johnny ran from the orchard toward the Keep's house around the corner to tell Mrs. Keep what happened. Mrs. Keep dashed to meet her girls. She scooped Hitty up in her arms to carry her the rest of the way home.

After a drink of water fresh from the well, Mrs. Keep placed some clean rags soaked in cider vinegar onto Hitty's stings to reduce the pain and swelling. This made Hitty feel better, but Johnny imagined that she would never again want to see another bee as long as she lived. She probably wasn't too eager to see sheep either!

Bees!

Putting Pen to Paper

Not every day was as exciting as that day in Mr. Forsyth's orchard. Back in the cool darkness of Colonel Hale's shop, the boys kept working at Johnny's lessons. Once the boys made their way through enough newspaper advertisements about missing farm animals, as well as stories about lightning strikes and children falling into wells, Nicholas felt Johnny was ready to move on from reading to writing.

He continued to be a patient and kind teacher to his friend. Because of that, Johnny felt safe making the kinds of mistakes that all new readers and writers make. When he mis-

pronounced words, Nicholas didn't laugh—although both boys collapsed in a puddle of giggles when he read the word "pretty" as "purty" because it just sounded funny. That became a joke of theirs for days and days.

"Nicholas, I need a break," Johnny would say when he was feeling restless or was making too many mistakes.

"Okay. Want to go see if anyone is playing outside?" his wise little instructor would say. A break always helped everyone come back and focus. After they stretched their legs enough, they'd head back to get a cup of cider and maybe a cookie from Phillis. Then Nicholas and Johnny would sit to read again.

Johnny was getting so good at reading print that he could make out the labels on items in the store and titles on books on the shelves.

One day, Nicholas had Johnny sit on a cider barrel at the counter. He cleared off a space to lay a thick piece of paper, a small inkpot, and a quill pen cut from a goose feather.

Nicholas stood next to him and used a ruler and pencil to make faint, straight lines across the paper.

"Johnny," he said, "I know you're ready to do some writing now. This is how I learned. First you learn reading, then you learn writing."

Phillis, who was in her sewing room off the store, poked her head out of the door. "Smart boy, Nicholas! Johnny, you've got a good teacher there. Wonder where he learned all these smart things from?" She chuckled, and the boys laughed as well.

"Miss Phillis, did you teach Nicholas to read?" Johnny asked.

"I did," she answered. "Not in a shop like this, but in the kitchen over at Reverend Williams' house. That was one job I did not mind at all. I taught him by using the Primer book, just like I used in someone else's kitchen when I was young. It was important for everyone in Reverend Williams' house to know how to read so we could read the Bible. He was the minister, after all."

"Do you still read it?" asked Johnny.

"Sure do," she replied. "When we left as free people from Reverend Williams' house, I didn't have much. But I had Nicholas, my sewing supplies, my bedsheets, and a Bible. That's all I really needed. With that, I could make a home anywhere." She gazed quietly in Nicholas' direction. "Nicholas always learned so quickly. I might have helped him learn to read, but it was Nicholas who helped me learn to write."

Phillis told Johnny that she'd never learned to write since no one ever thought it was important to teach her. Nicholas had learned to write from one of Reverend Williams' grandsons. He practiced and practiced and practiced on his own when he could find time away from his work at the Williams' house.

When Colonel and Mrs. Hale asked Phillis if she would like to work for them as a seamstress for the store—sewing on buttons and making trousers and coats for the men who had no one to do that kind of work for them—she agreed. She and Nicholas rented a room of their own. She got to keep the money made from selling her work at the store, and she and Nicholas were welcome to share the kitchen with the Hales.

Nicholas was eager to learn the work of

a merchant. He loved the store. He loved the variety of people that passed through negotiating prices and bartering goods and services.

"Phillis, do you remember what I told you when you first started with a quill and ink?" Nicholas called to her.

"Sure do. Use a light touch—not too much ink on the tip—and start simple. Make straight lines and then move on to round letters: small o's and small a's and small e's, and shapes like that. Fill up a page with them before moving on to anything else."

So, that's what they did. As much as Johnny wanted to jump straight to learning to write his name in cursive, that was not the way he learned. On the afternoons when he and Nicholas worked together in between morning chores and evening chores, lots of blank pages of scrap paper were filled with straight lines and swoops and circles. When Johnny felt he had a good sense of how to grip the quill and not make too many splotches with the dark, wet ink, they moved to round letters, then letters with lines up (b's, d's, f's, t's) and letters with tails down (g's and p's and q's). The first capital letters he learned were J and C, and then he was able to attempt J-o-h-n and C-h-a-p-m-a-n. It was difficult to get them all attached like Nicholas could, but his wise young friend promised him that would come with practice.

"Nicholas, why did Phillis want to learn how to write, even though she's already grown?" Johnny asked.

"Well, since we came here, Phillis wanted to be able to keep records about the work she did, or had to do, and about how much she got paid or was owed. She had never had to do anything like that before. So, I told her I could show her some of what I know. She'd already figured out some of the basic arithmetic from running the kitchen at Reverend Williams' house. All she needed was enough tutoring with the writing to keep her own accounts. And I don't mind sharing what I've learned. I might not have much, but I have learning and it doesn't cost anything to share it."

And that was yet another lesson Johnny learned in his time with Nicholas—the importance of sharing the gifts you had with others, no matter how small they seemed.

Nathaniel's Jam

Since spending more time on the green and at Colonel Hale's shop, Johnny's days had become very full. Mornings and evenings, though, were still for the farm and his family, including his little brother, Nathaniel. His father was busy on their small farm and building the new minister's house. Mother Lucy's endless work within the house to keep them all clean, fed, and dressed kept her busy from sunrise to sundown. Johnny helped wherever he was needed. This was true for most children in towns like Longmeadow in the early years after the War of Independence. Soldiers who had been away for a long time were eager to get back to life with their families at home.

Johnny's days had a predictable routine. Sunday was the Sabbath and that meant going to church for most of the day. Every other day was spent at home and on the green, but mornings and late afternoons were for chores and Nathaniel. While Eda Keep brought Hitty everywhere she went, Nathaniel was still too young to make the trip to the green on his chubby little legs without getting too tired. Instead, Johnny was asked to keep him busy at home until naptime. Then Johnny was free to be on his own for a while.

Strawberry picking was a favorite chore for both boys. Berry bushes could be found all through the woods near their house. Johnny made sure to give Nathaniel his own basket to collect with so he wouldn't be jealous of Johnny's.

Mother Lucy would say, "Now remember, Johnny, don't let him eat too many straight from the bush. He'll end up with a stomachache. Do you hear that, Nathaniel? Not too many!"

"I hear that, Mama!" Nathaniel said with a twinkle in his eye.

"That's good," said Mother Lucy. "And remember, if you bring enough home, I can make some nice strawberry jam for our biscuits." Fresh strawberry jam was one of the best parts of summer!

Johnny led his little brother along the

edges of the woods near their home and the road down to the river in search of the small, red treats hiding among the low, green leaves. Different seasons brought different treasures to Longmeadow's woods and fields. Early summer was for berries, and Johnny and Nathaniel loved it. Blueberries and raspberries and strawberries and blackberries—all were wonderful to eat, picked fresh and warm from the bushes and wonderful in Mother Lucy's pies, tarts, and jams.

One morning, Nathaniel gave Johnny quite a scare when he disappeared from sight. Mother Lucy had taken a walk to Grandmother Cooley's house with Baby Abner to borrow some flour, and she left Johnny to keep an eye on Nathaniel. Johnny had been practicing his handwriting in the dirt with a stick while Nathaniel ran back and forth chattering to himself.

"Nate, come sit with me. Look, let's make pictures in the dirt. Here's a stick for you." But making shapes in the dirt with a stick didn't hold the toddler's attention for long and he scampered away.

Johnny was working hard to link the C with h-a-p and the m-a-n to spell out his last name when he realized it was all of a sudden too quiet. He didn't know where Nathaniel was. He called his name.

"Nate?" No answer. He called again, and again there was no answer. Immediately Johnny jumped up from the ground and scanned his surroundings. No sign of Nathaniel.

"Nathaniel? Where'd you go?" He checked behind the hanging laundry and inside the barrel in the garden. Nothing. He ran to the elm tree out front calling his name. Nothing. Johnny's heart pumped harder with fear.

"Nathaniel!!!" He called out more loudly while trying to keep his voice pleasant so as to not scare his little brother. If Nathaniel thought he was in trouble, he might try to hide.

"Nathaniel! Wow! Look what I found!" Johnny called, even though he hadn't actually found anything interesting. He was just trying to lure the toddler out through curiosity.

Johnny wondered where to go first. The house? The woods? The well? That was his biggest fear since everyone knew that little children Nathaniel's age often drowned after falling into wells.

    He decided he must run first to the well. Time mattered the most there. He set off quickly across the yard to the well, filling with dread as he ran. Peering down into the darkness, Johnny saw that the well seemed quiet and undisturbed. The bucket was still raised, and all was still. He quickly scanned the dirt around the well. No signs of Nathaniel's little footprints. Thank goodness!

    He looked around again, calling Nathaniel's name more nervously now. Where to next? Cooley Brook? Oh no! Running at full speed, Johnny ran through the woods, calling for his little brother and constantly scanning the bushes and trees for clues about where he might be. Reaching the brook, he found no signs of Nathaniel. Slightly relieved, he raced back toward his house. Was it time to let Mother Lucy know? Or should he check the house first?

    "House first and then I'll go for help," he decided.

Running into the house, Johnny hoped to find Nathaniel playing with the wooden bowls he liked to stack. But he wasn't. Johnny called his name again but heard nothing in return. That's when he noticed the large red stain on the floor. He stood with his mind racing. What was that? Surely it hadn't been there before. Mother Lucy would never leave anything untidy in their little home before setting out.

Nothing seemed disturbed or out of place as Johnny glanced around. He then noticed a trail of smaller red drops leading to a tiny red handprint on the wooden floor by the

The jam pot

bed. Tossing up the corner of the bed's coverlet, Johnny heard a giggle. The faint shape of Nathaniel's chubby little body and plentiful head of curls lay in the darkness on the small trundle bed tucked under their parents' larger bed.

Johnny yanked the trundle out from under the bed as Nathaniel squealed in delight. He clutched a small crock, his hands and mouth covered in strawberry jam. The sticky jam was everywhere! The floor, the sheets, his clothes, his hair—all bore signs of strawberry jam. Johnny had never been so relieved to find such a mess in his life!

"There you are! Why didn't you answer me when I called you? You scared me half to death!" Johnny took the crock of mostly-eaten jam from his brother's sticky hands.

"Surprise!" cried Nathaniel.

"Yes, you surprised me all right. Mother Lucy is going to be in for quite a surprise, too, if she comes home and sees the mess you've made." Johnny pulled Nathaniel out from the trundle bed and set him on the floor.

"Now don't touch anything!" Johnny

brought his little brother outside to clean him up with fresh water. He washed the jam off his face and hands, out of his hair, and quickly changed his clothes. Johnny handed his brother a soapy rag and made sure to keep an extra-close eye on him while he cleaned up the mess inside. Johnny hoped that Mother Lucy would just be happy that a lost container of strawberry jam was not as bad as a lost little boy.

The Trundle Bed

The School Teacher

"She's here! She's here! She's here!" Eda chirped as she ran up to Johnny, who was on his way to meet Nicholas. Hitty, of course, followed closely behind.

"Who's here?" Johnny asked as he was pulled abruptly from his daydreaming.

"The new schoolmistress! She's here! I saw her trunk being brought into the Hale's house this morning. My goodness, Johnny, I'm so excited!"

"Oh," said Johnny, who definitely didn't share his friend's enthusiasm.

"She's so young and pretty. I just know she's going to be a wonderful teacher for our school. I can tell already that she is kind. Nicholas is so lucky that he will be living in the same house as her. I am so jealous. I bet they get to have all their meals together. Imagine… having breakfast with a teacher!"

Actually, Johnny wasn't quite sure he could

imagine that with the same joy Eda had.

"Are you on your way to go see Nicholas now? Do you mind if Hitty and I tag along? Maybe she will be in the store and I can meet her. I have ever so many questions I'd like to ask. Is she the kind of teacher that comes outside to join the children's games? Has she ever kept a school before? Does she plan on being strict? Will she come back next summer or does she plan on getting married?"

"That sure is a lot of questions," Johnny said. "You might want to save some for another time."

"You are so funny, Johnny!" Eda said with a laugh.

Johnny wasn't exactly sure what he had said that was funny, though. If he knew he was going to have to talk to someone, he'd often plan out a question or two to ask since talking to people often made him a little nervous.

"Are you going to see Nicholas? Can we come with you?" Eda asked.

"Sure," said Johnny as she grabbed him by the hand and hurried him along.

Johnny, Eda and Hitty entered the side

door to Colonel Hale's shop and found all quiet. There was no sign of anyone about. But from the room off the back of the shop came the sound of voices.

Eda poked Johnny forward, encouraging him to go around the counter and into the room. When he didn't, she cleared her throat loudly. No one came to greet them. She tried again. Still nothing. Finally, Eda opened and closed the door to the shop again—loudly.

That did the trick. Mrs. Hale poked her head around the half-opened parlor door to find the three children standing in the shop.

"Oh, look who's here! Hello there, children! Come here, come here! I have someone I'd like to introduce you to!"

Eda nudged Johnny forward and pulled Hitty along by the hand. They walked around the counter into the parlor.

There, on a carpeted floor, amidst shiny, polished parlor furniture and gold-colored, floor-length curtains, stood Miss Polly Reynolds, the new schoolmistress. She was about eighteen years old, wearing a simple blue cotton dress with a pink floral petticoat peeking out. Her soft brown curls were swept back neatly under a white cap, and she wore a black ribbon around her neck. Eda was awestruck.

"Miss Reynolds, I'd like to introduce you to three of your future students. This is Editha and Mehittable Keep, who live just down the street. And here is Johnny Chapman, who lives past the north end of the green."

Eda and Hitty curtsied toward the new teacher, and Johnny nodded his head down in a slightly awkward bow. He never did feel comfortable making a bow.

"Well, hello. It's so nice to make your acquaintance, children," Miss Reynolds replied, curtsying in return. It was then that Johnny had a chance to notice Nicholas and Miss Phillis in the room as well, having also just been introduced to Miss Reynolds.

Mrs. Hale said, "Phillis, I think this would be the perfect time for us to get some refreshments. Would you mind helping me get some from the kitchen? We can all get better acquainted then. You children have a seat. We won't be long at all."

"Of course," said Phillis as the two women exited the parlor.

Johnny rarely had a chance to sit in a room as nice as this one. His own home was so simple. Two rooms below, and a loft above. Colonel Hale's house, however, was elegant and spacious. Besides having a shop located in the side addition, he had two parlors, a dining room, a study on the main floor, a kitchen at the rear, and a wide staircase leading to several bed chambers on the second floor.

Miss Reynolds sat in one of the soft armchairs while the four children settled themselves in the heavily polished side chairs with carved feet and pink satin cushions. Hitty's feet were nowhere near touching the floor. Johnny's feet, he suddenly realized, were bare...and filthy. He'd forgotten to wear his shoes today! And here he was, sitting in a fine-looking parlor meeting his teacher for the first time. He was so embarrassed. He did his best to tuck his dirty feet as far as possible under his seat. Why hadn't he remembered to carry his shoes with him to the green this time!?! Mother Lucy was busy with the bread baking and hadn't even looked up when he left the house.

"...is that so, Johnny?" someone asked from outside his thoughts. He sat still, quickly

Hale's parlor

trying to figure out who had spoken to him. He realized all eyes were on him. Eda's intense gaze in particular indicated he should answer Miss Reynolds.

"Um, yes," he answered quickly, though he wasn't sure exactly what the question was.

"Ah, I have two younger brothers myself. I know how much responsibility…and commotion…that can be," Miss Reynolds replied.

Phew, so it must've been about his little brothers, Johnny realized. Thank goodness he had answered correctly. Dirty feet and not hearing the question! Johnny feared he was not off to a great start with Miss Reynolds.

Thankfully, though, when Mrs. Hale returned with tea and biscuits, she held up most of the conversation with Miss Reynolds. Eda could always be counted on to answer for the children when a question or comment was thrown their way. Phillis asked Miss Reynolds her thoughts on whether or not Nicholas should attend school.

"Nicholas seems to think his time would be better spent around the shop reading on his own," Phillis said. "He supposes he already knows everything he needs to know from school— even though he's never been."

Nicholas kept his gaze firmly locked on the carpet, as if some fascinating swirl of wool fibers was the most interesting thing in the world.

"Is that so, Nicholas?" Miss Reynolds asked him. "Do you like to read?"

"Yes, ma'am," he said, his gaze releasing from the carpet.

Tea and biscuits

"I do, too. Would you tell me more about what you like to read?" Miss Reynolds asked.

Nicholas told her of the newspapers and almanac. "And also Gulliver's Travels, anything by Benjamin Franklin, and other kinds of books that come through the shop. As long as I don't mark them up or make creases, Colonel Hale doesn't mind if I read the books on the shelves."

"Wow, that certainly is quite a lot! And you understand and enjoy what you are reading?"

"Yes, Miss Reynolds, I do," Nicholas responded. "I like writing, too, but I don't have a reason to do much of that. Someday I'd like to be a printer and a writer like Benjamin Franklin and have my own shop. That way I could spend my whole day just surrounded by words and pages."

"That does sound wonderful! I've always appreciated Mr. Franklin's clever mind myself," she replied. "And what about arithmetic? Have you much experience with numbers and mathematics?"

"Well, I've been learning to make my

way in Colonel Hale's account books. I help to keep track of customers' debts and credits. And I help Phillis keep track of her accounts as well. I don't know that there is much more to know about arithmetic besides that. Is there?"

"Ah, there is indeed," said Miss Reynolds. "And, yes, it does seem that you have a strong foundation in arithmetic. But, Nicholas, I do believe school could help you go further toward seeing and understanding the wider world of numbers. I bet Mr. Franklin himself would agree that arithmetic helped him in his scientific experiments."

Nicholas considered this quite seriously.

Phillis spoke up. "Seems to me that you do have more room for learning in that head of yours, Nicholas."

"I agree," said Miss Reynolds. "I think a scholar like you could be a real inspiration to others in the classroom. We have brand new spelling books to use this term by Mr. Noah Webster. Our school is getting its very own set, and anyone who comes will be the first to use them. They are the first schoolbooks written by an American for American students. You may find lots of new material in there for your mind. And formal instruction in arithmetic can be quite different from learning by experience. That's important as well, of course, but there is much to be learned beyond that if you would like."

"Plus, you can spend more time with Johnny and me and play games during recess! You don't get recess unless you go to school," Eda chimed in.

That made everyone laugh. Eda was absolutely right!

Johnny left the Hale's parlor that afternoon with two impressions: first, as much as shoes made him uncomfortable, formal parlors made him more uncomfortable.

And second, Miss Reynolds was going to be a much better teacher for him than Master Loomis.

The Hale's house

First Day

The morning of the first day of school dawned as any other ordinary day would, though it was certainly not an ordinary day for Johnny. The sun rose through the east-facing windows of the Chapman family's small house in tones of gold and pink. The first to stir was always the baby and Mother Lucy, who woke to start the fire for the day.

She was followed by Captain Chapman, whose heavier footsteps always seemed to shake the walls and floors. That woke little Nathaniel, who slept snuggled next to Johnny on the trundle bed.

"Johnny, you 'wake?" Nathaniel would whisper loudly into his sleepy brother's face. On this particular day, Johnny was actually awake before all of them, his stomach feeling like a thousand grasshoppers bounced around inside of it.

In the light of early dawn, he dressed for

School desks at the ready

the day, making sure both shoes and his stockings were lined up by the door so he wouldn't forget them when he left. As the others began to wake and move about for the day's business, those grasshoppers seemed to jump about more and more. After morning chores and breakfast were done, it was time for Johnny to put on those shoes and head toward the brick schoolhouse on the green for the first day of summer term.

"Johnny, I packed you a special lunch for your first day: some bread, cheese, fresh raspberries, pickles, and some oatmeal cookies. Maybe you can even share them with your friends."

"Thank you," said Johnny, who wondered if he'd even have an appetite at all by then. He'd had none at all for the breakfast porridge made special today with a spoonful of apple butter. Nathaniel's soft, chubby fingers grabbed hold of Johnny's hand and asked if he could go to school with him.

"Sorry, Nate. You have to be four years old to go to school." Nathaniel scowled and pouted as he gripped Johnny's hand harder.

"I AM four!" Nathaniel said strongly. "See? I AM." He let go of Johnny's hand to stand as tall and as straight as he could. This only made everyone chuckle.

"Not for another year," said Johnny. "Don't worry, Nate," Captain Chapman spoke up. "Your time will come soon enough. But for now, your mother and Baby Abner need your help around the house. You can be the big brother while Johnny is away during the day." That idea distracted Nathaniel from his pouting for a little bit at least. And with that, Johnny went off to give school another try.

As Johnny set out for the main road, he saw his cousin, Willie Cooley, heading out as well. Aunt Abiel licked her fingers to smooth his hair down. Willie grimaced as he tried to pull away. Nobody liked to have their hair fixed that way!

Willie broke free the instant he saw Johnny. He met him on the side of the road, leaving Aunt Abiel throwing her hands up in exasperation.

"Ugh," Willie said as he ran his own

fingers through his hair trying to rustle it back into its natural state of untidiness. "Don't you hate when they do that!?!"

Both Johnny and Willie were the only children in their families going to school this term - Johnny because he was the oldest and only one of school age, and Willie because he was the youngest and only one of school age.

"I tell ya, I'm glad they're letting me go to school this term," Willie said. "Sam and Simeon have to work the fields with Uncle Jabe, and my sister is fifteen now so she doesn't have to go anymore. But I like school—especially math. I'm hoping we get a teacher this term who gives lots and lots of math problems. I'd much rather sit all day at school than be on the farm with my brothers telling me every little thing they think I'm doing wrong. No, thank you!"

"I'm just hoping it's better than last term," said Johnny. "I already met the teacher. She seems better than Master Loomis. I bet you'll like her."

Johnny and Nicholas had arranged that they would meet up before heading into the brick schoolhouse. This was to be Nicholas' first time ever in school. Both boys and Willie were dressed in their best and nicest clothes for the first day. Nicholas didn't need to bring a lunch because he could just go right home and eat during lunch break since it was so near the school.

Children were already gathered outside the school building. Miss Reynolds arrived early to make sure everything was in order. The school had only one room, and Miss Reynolds was the only teacher.

Eda Keep came running up to the boys the moment she spotted them. Hitty, for once, was nowhere to be seen. She had found some younger playmates all her own. Eda was with Flavia Bliss, Annie Williams, and Lucinda Colton. Johnny recognized all of them from spending long Sundays sitting for church services at the meetinghouse. Just as they did at church, Eda said they all planned to sit together in school—as long as Miss Reynolds let them.

Johnny hadn't even thought about what the seating arrangement might be. Would he and Nicholas be separated?

They would have the chance to find out now since Miss Reynolds came out and rang a bell calling school to order. The children formed two lines to enter—one for boys and one for girls. As they did so, Johnny caught a glimpse of the Burt sisters sitting on their front steps, watching from down the street. He wasn't quite sure if he was jealous of them for their family's choice not to send them to the brick schoolhouse, or if he felt sorry for them. They clearly looked as if they might enjoy the company of so many other children.

Many of the returning students knew exactly how the seating worked: youngest in the front, oldest in the back; girls on one side, boys on the other. Nicholas and Johnny hesitated, as was their nature, and waited for the initial scramble and excitement to subside. Then they spied an empty bench just past the middle of the room and took seats side by side.

Although students could attend school until they were fourteen years old, Johnny and Nicholas were among the oldest boys there that day. Summer term meant that boys older than ten or eleven were needed at home to work on their family's farm. This suited Johnny just fine because part of what had made him feel so unhappy over winter term was the teasing from the older boys. He wouldn't miss them one bit.

Miss Reynolds called the room to order and the excited murmurings ceased. The bright eyes of the eager students and the solemn eyes of the more nervous children all fixed their gaze on her.

"Good day, children. My name is Miss Reynolds. I will be your teacher for the next twelve weeks. We have much to do and much to learn, not just about reading, writing, and arithmetic, but also about each other as citizens of this schoolhouse, Longmeadow, and our new nation."

The children sat in rapt attention.

"In order to begin our important work, we must first find out who we have among us this term. I will call you to my desk one at a time. You will tell me your name, age, and how much schooling you have had. When it is not your turn, I expect you to sit quietly looking over whatever books you may have brought with you. If you have not brought any with you, please look on with a neighbor."

And with that, the summer term in the brick schoolhouse had begun.

Miss Reynolds began attendance with the youngest students—the "abecedarians" as they were called since they were just learning their ABCs. Among this group was Hitty. Each child was handed a well-worn copy of the New England Primer and told to spend some time looking through its pages quietly. The Primer taught letters and letter sounds, and it contained pictures, poems, and prayers all students were expected to learn.

Miss Reynolds made her way through the six- and seven-year-olds next. Johnny knew his turn would be coming soon. The grasshoppers from the early morning were back in his stomach. Miss Reynolds called him by name and he approached.

"Good morning, Johnny, so nice to see you here this morning."

"Thank you, Miss Reynolds."

"Now Johnny, let me enter you in my roster so we can officially get you registered. J-o-h-n C-h-a-p-m-a-n. Is that correct?"

"Yes, miss," he answered.

"And you prefer to be called 'Johnny'?"

"Yes, miss."

"And, Johnny, how old are you?"

"Eight years old, miss."

"Thank you. I know we spoke some at the Hale's house, but can you tell me how much schooling you have had?"

"Well, I've mostly just learned at home, Miss Reynolds. Both here with my stepmother and some when I was living in Leominster with my grandparents."

"Is that so?" she asked.

"I did come to school last winter for a few weeks, but my father thought it better to keep me home after a while."

"Well, I hope you will be able to stay with us all term," she said with a smile. "Johnny, I'd like to hear you read for me so that I can get a sense of where you should begin in our new books. Please take this new Speller, turn to page fourteen, and begin reading at the top of the page for me."

As Johnny took the book, a familiar nervousness washed over him. Reading with Nicholas was one thing, but in front of the teacher was another. Even though the students were supposed to be busy with their own work and not paying attention to him, there was no doubt that many were secretly focused on what was happening at the teacher's desk.

Webster's American Spelling Book

The book, with its blue cover, was new and stiff. It made a soft crack sound when he opened it fully. He turned to page fourteen, not knowing what he would find. To his surprise, the words took shape and meaning before his eyes. He read aloud from Rules for Conduct in the Classroom.

"He that speaks loudly in school will not learn his own book well, nor let the others in theirs; but those that make no noise will soon be wise, and gain much love and goodwill."

"Very good indeed, Johnny." Miss Reynolds praised him in a soft voice. He couldn't help but smile. "Those are wise words, aren't they? And I'm sure they will serve you well while in the schoolroom. You may go back to your seat now. Take this book with you and see if you can memorize those lines and be prepared to share them when I call you to recite after lunch. Have Nicholas come to me next, please."

At lunchtime, Johnny kicked off his shoes and ran freely around the grass on the green, happy to be out in the open air. Several boys his age ran and chased each other, stretching their legs playing tag. After sitting still for so long it felt good to just run!

Recess lasted for a full hour, giving those who lived close enough to the school time to go home and eat, and those who didn't have time to find a shady spot to relax and enjoy their lunches brought from home. Nicholas offered to have Johnny come home with him, but on this first day, Johnny just wanted to be outside. Willie Cooley and another Cooley cousin, Lewis, stayed too, and they all ate and played together. It seemed no time at all before the nearby children had returned from their houses ready to have some fun before they all went back into the schoolhouse.

The afternoon passed quickly. Miss Reynolds went over the rules and expectations for behavior in the classroom, listened to some recitations, and told the students about an exciting event that would happen at the end of the term.

In the warmth of the late May afternoon, some of the youngest children fell asleep on the benches. Miss Reynolds let them sleep while she told the older students about

"Incorporation Day." Longmeadow had been a part of the larger town of Springfield for more than a hundred years, but Springfield had grown so big and busy that Longmeadow residents decided they wanted to be an independent town. That way they could elect their own leaders, collect their own taxes for projects, and make their own decisions. Their petition was successful, and now they would be the first town in Massachusetts to be incorporated since the war ended.

This was cause for a celebration, and the town leaders asked if the schoolchildren would prepare a presentation. The whole town would be there, with a parade and music and dancing and speeches and contests of all kinds, and lots and lots of food. Longmeadow had never had this kind of celebration before, and it would be exciting to be a part of it.

At the end of the first school day, Johnny returned home with stories to tell, a cookie from Mrs. Hale to bring to Nathaniel, and a new confidence in his heart.

And he was ready for more.

School Days

As the days grew hotter throughout June and into July, the children of the brick schoolhouse did their best to keep cool as they worked through their studies. The windows were opened to allow for a breeze, and the students made trips to the well for cool drinks of water. Miss Reynolds let them take their lessons outdoors and under the trees when the building became too stuffy.

Johnny progressed so nicely in his penmanship that he was asked to show some younger children in the class how to get started, just as Nicholas had shown him. And Nicholas was making good use of his time working through the arithmetic book. Having mastered multiplication and division, he was making his very own copybook of all the arithmetic rules that he'd learned—skills that would help him if he ever had a business of his own. It was a beautiful book, with a hand-made, marbled paper cover and pages filled with Nicholas' neatest cursive. Not a stray ink blot could be seen anywhere. Willie Cooley worked on one, too.

One drowsy morning, while the abecedarians droned on in reciting their vowel sounds—"a-b, ab, e-b, eb, i-b, ib, o-b, ob, u-b,

Josie comes to school

ub"—Johnny's thoughts wandered far from the classroom. He was thinking of a bird's nest he had seen on the ground while walking to school. Fallen nests always made him feel sad because he knew the hard work the bird put into building a safe and comfortable home for its little ones. There was no sign this morning of broken eggs or fallen baby birds, but it still made him wonder what happened to the bird family that lived in it. Perhaps it was disturbed by the wind, or perhaps by a curious (and hungry) critter.

Johnny picked it up carefully and placed it back in the crook of the highest tree branch he could reach—which wasn't nearly as high as it needed to be—and hoped that the bird family might return while he was at school.

This was what Johnny was wondering about when a surprising snort and splash of warm wetness struck his neck. Looking over his shoulder, he gasped to realize a large red cow was staring straight at him through the opened window, its head fully in the classroom. The whole class turned at the sound to see the cow. Its white-spotted muzzle chewed a mouthful of green grass, slowly and loudly turning it over in its mouth with its long, pink tongue.

"Josie!" Beulah Booth called out. "What are you doing here!?!"

Up Beulah jumped and ran outside to collect her family's enormous cow. It was a funny sight to see little Beulah grab the giant creature by the rope dangling from her neck and try to pull her in the direction of home. Josie didn't budge. She seemed much more interested in the tall grass outside the schoolhouse window than in listening to poor, mortified Beulah. Beulah tugged and tugged, and Josie chewed and chewed.

Sticking her head outside the schoolhouse window, Miss Reynolds suggested, "Beulah, perhaps it would be better to run home and fetch one of your older brothers to come collect Josie. She seems quite content here and perhaps would be a good audience for some of the younger students' recitations."

All the children, even poor Beulah, had a good laugh at this.

Funny distractions—like the one Josie

offered—aside, Johnny's school days had taken on a predictable routine. Mornings were for study and work, noontime was for recess and games, and afternoons were for preparing for Incorporation Day. Without a doubt, Johnny's favorite part was recess.

Since returning to school, Johnny had met so many new children. Most of them became friends, but try as he might, he just couldn't make peace with one: Margaret Pratt. At twelve years old, Margaret was one of the older students in school. Her sister, Almira, was tolerable, but Margaret was terrible. She poked the little ones until they cried, pulled out the hair ribbon of any girl passing by then "accidentally" stepped on it in the dirt, and blamed the boys for spilling ink she knew she had spilled herself. You never wanted to send Margaret to the well to fill the water bucket because you never knew what she would do to it on the way back.

Johnny and Nicholas did their best to stay as far away as possible, but not Eda Keep. Eda wasn't intimidated by Margaret's bullying one bit.

One day, Margaret set her sights on teasing Hitty. Everyone knew Hitty was terrified of bees. Ever since the stinging incident in Mr. Forsyth's orchard, there was nothing anyone could say that would make Hitty understand why such a creature had any business in the world. Butterflies, fireflies, caterpillars, ladybugs, dragonflies, and even ants were fine. But bees? They were just villains with stingers! Johnny tried to explain to her that flowers and fruits needed bees to carry their pollen to make more flowers and more fruits. And the honey that Hitty liked so much on her cakes was all because of bees. Hitty was willing to give it all up if it meant no more bees and no more bee stings.

On this particular day, just before morning recess, Johnny looked up from his speller to find Margaret doing something peculiar. Following her gaze toward the window, Johnny noticed she was watching a big, fat, fuzzy bumblebee slowly buzzing around the inside of the windowpane. As the bee gently bumped into the glass over and over again, Johnny imagined that the bee clearly wished it were outside instead of in. While the middle grades droned on with their recitations, Margaret quietly got up from her seat and trapped the bee in her handkerchief. She grinned as she felt the bulge of the bee in her handkerchief.

"Poor creature," Johnny whispered. Nicholas looked toward his friend to see what troubled him. Johnny simply pointed at Margaret. "She trapped a bumblebee."

Margaret scanned the room wondering what to do with her new pet. Her eyes landed on little Hitty Keep. Margaret smiled to herself and patted the loosely folded handkerchief on her desk. Soon, Miss Reynolds called for morning recess and the class clamored outside for some free time.

Johnny watched as Margaret picked up her handkerchief, inspected her fuzzy treasure inside, and showed it to her friend, Martha. She whispered a dastardly plan into Martha's ear as both girls snickered. As Johnny went to the back of the room to get the rope he brought to play jump rope, he wondered what trouble they were planning. From the doorway, he saw Margaret and Martha.

Nicholas said, "Well, there goes trouble. I'd better warn Eda."

"Oh, Hitty!" Margaret called.

Hitty paused in her playing with the younger girls to look at Margaret.

"Me?" Hitty asked incredulously. What on earth could Margaret want with her?

"Yes, of course you," Margaret replied. "Miss Reynolds said you did such a nice job at your recitations this morning that she wanted me to give you a special surprise."

"Really?" Hitty asked dubiously, still wondering why an older girl like Margaret might be talking to her.

"Yes, silly! Would I lie to you?"

"Well, what is it?"

"You have to close your eyes and open your hands like this," she instructed, forming her hands into a cup. And just like that, Johnny knew what Margaret had planned. Never one to raise his voice, though, he stood frozen trying to figure out what to do.

"Why do I have to close my eyes?" Hitty asked.

"I don't know," said Margaret. "I guess you should always close your eyes for a surprise, right? It makes it more exciting."

"And Miss Reynolds told you to give it to me?" Hitty asked.

"Yes, of course. Stop asking so many questions! Do you want it or not?"

"I guess so?" replied Hitty, though she didn't sound so sure.

"Good. Now close your eyes and put out your hands."

"No, Hitty, don't listen to her!" Johnny said. But it was too late, and his voice too quiet.

By this point, Nicholas had found Eda and told her that Margaret was planning a trick on her sister. Eda knew that was not a good thing. She stood across the yard carefully watching as Hitty scrunched up her eyes and held her hands out in front of her.

Margaret opened the handkerchief into Hitty's hands. Even though Eda could not see what Margaret put in her sister's hands, she could hear the screeching and see her arms frantically swatting at her dress as she ran in circles.

"Get it off! Get it off! Get it off! Get it off," Hitty screamed as Margaret laughed.

Eda ran to her sister as Hitty screamed, "It's a bee! Get it off! Get it off!"

Eda held her still, examining her all over, checking the folds of her dress and ruffles of her sleeves, and even the braids on her head.

"It's gone, Hitty. It's gone, it's gone. I don't see it anywhere. It's gone."

Poor Hitty, red-faced and sweaty with hot tears streaming down her face, didn't know what to do. Eda held her close and told her it was all over, and she was unharmed. Then, turning her attention to Margaret, Eda filled with rage.

"What did you do to my sister!?!"

"Oh, please," said Margaret. "It's just a little joke."

"You are horrible, Margaret! Why do you have to be so MEAN!?! Does it make you feel good to make someone else feel bad? You don't have to be that way!"

"Gosh, it's a joke, Eda. Look around. See? Everyone else is laughing."

Eda did not look around. She kept her attention focused on Margaret. Her eyes blazed with anger. But Johnny did look around, and he could see that, yes, a few kids laughed, but most kids did not, including him and Nicholas. Not everyone else was laughing. Hitty was crying. Eda was fuming.

"Actually, Margaret—" Johnny spoke up, finding his voice stronger.

The Brick Schoolhouse

"What!?!"

"Um, I'm not laughing," he said. "That was mean to Hitty. It's not funny to watch someone be mean to someone littler and quieter. It's just…mean."

"Oh, please, I was trying to help her. Those kinds of bees hardly ever sting. I wanted her to see how friendly they are. Thought maybe she could keep it as a pet and learn to not be so scared of them."

But Johnny wasn't done. "Plus, it was mean to that poor bee, too. It wasn't bothering anyone, and then next thing it knows someone's yelling and swatting at it."

"Shut up, Johnny. No one asked you," said Margaret.

"Why don't you shut up, Margaret!" Eda hollered. Eda never had a hard time finding her voice. "I've had more than enough of you and your bullying. I should have said something long ago, but I didn't. But now you've gone too far! I'm going inside right now to tell Miss Reynolds, and we'll see what kind of punishment she gives you."

"Oh, please, Miss Reynolds loves me.

Besides, nothing bad happened. She didn't get stung. Miss Reynolds will just be mad at you for tattling."

"It's not tattling if someone hurts someone else. And you hurt my sister, and you hurt people's feelings here all the time. You might not hurt people with your fists, but you hurt them every day with your words, your nasty little looks, and your 'jokes'," Eda said.

That afternoon, Margaret spent two hours copying over and over again onto four pages: "To my schoolmates I will be kind and peaceable. I will not scare them. I will not quarrel with them or tease them. I will behave toward them as I would like them to behave toward me."

Miss Reynolds tacked one page of writing on the wall at the front of the room, one copy on the wall next to Margaret's desk, and one copy by the door to be seen before recess. She also sent one copy home with Margaret to be signed by a parent. Now, certainly, she would have enough reminders.

The Meetinghouse

Lightning Strikes

Walking home from school one day in August, Johnny dragged under the weight of the hot and humid air. The dirt felt hot under his bare feet, so he kept to the grass as much as he could. Even the rooster weathervane atop the meetinghouse seemed to be melting. Miss Reynolds had dismissed school an hour early because there was no way to find any relief from the heat and humidity. The Incorporation Day Celebration was just a week away, and each class level had been rehearsing their bit, but with little success and little interest. It was just too hot to do anything.

All Johnny could think of was hopping into the pond near his house to cool off. Longmeadow had many ponds, large and small, and just about any one of them would do right now.

At home, everyone was hot and bothered. Nathaniel was grumpy, baby Abner was screaming, and Mother Lucy was exasperated.

"Aw, thank goodness you're home early, Johnny. I could really use your help. Another set of hands. We are all at our wit's end with this weather. Come, off we go. Let's bring Nathaniel to splash around in the brook. We could all use a cooling off."

The water at the brook wasn't deep, but it was cool and pleasant and they all put their feet in. Johnny and Nathaniel splashed each other and giggled. It felt so good to get some relief from the stifling air. Mother Lucy even dangled Baby Abner's little feet in. He was four months old now and smiling and growing chubbier every day. The cool water startled him at first, but he soon sat in the brook with Mother Lucy's help, splashing his fists and kicking his feet. Everyone laughed along with him. Mother Lucy dipped her neckerchief in the water, wrung it out, and tied it around her neck again.

"I love this little brook, boys. The river is powerful and big and carries great boats loaded with cargo. Ponds are deep and still and full of fish, but a little brook in the woods, with its twisting ways and gentle waterfalls, is a treasure."

"I like it, too," said Johnny. "I've never seen where it starts, and I don't know where it goes, but I'd like to explore and find out someday."

"Me, too," said Nathaniel. "I 'splore with you, Johnny!"

"Of course, Nate. You can come with me," Johnny assured him. "Mother Lucy, do you know where the brook begins?"

"You know, I've lived here all my life, Johnny, and I've never really thought about where the brook comes from, but I do know where it goes. You can follow Cooley Brook down the hill as it winds around and meets up with the Connecticut River. I played in this brook when I was a girl. Now, my days are too busy with you boys and the house. My exploring days are over. You make sure you take the time to do some of that exploring while you're still young! And you'll have to let me know what you find!"

"Oh, I will. But for now, I think I'll stick to Cooley Brook."

That night, Johnny had a hard time falling asleep in the heat, especially as a thunder and lightning storm got closer. Some summer nights, Johnny would set up a bed outside, but his father told him tonight a big storm was likely to blow through, so it was best to stay inside. Such storms could be frightening, but Johnny knew they usually brought cooler air behind them. He eventually dozed off, only to be awakened by someone banging on the front door.

His father jumped out of bed to answer.

"Captain Chapman, fire on the green! All hands needed. Lightning strike to Ensign Williams' barn. Spreading to his house. The whole street is in danger!"

"On my way," Johnny's father replied. "Lucy, you stay here with the little ones. Johnny, you come with me. You're old enough to help."

Johnny was so startled he could hardly get his thoughts together as he jumped from his bed. They quickly dressed, grabbed some buckets, and ran out into the warm and humid night air.

The meetinghouse bell called people to come help. Ensign Williams lived right next door to the meetinghouse. Nicholas and Eda lived just a few houses to the south of him. Everyone had heard stories of fires started in chimneys, by fallen candles, or even by strikes of lightning, which quickly spread in places where wooden houses were close enough together. Embers flying from one fire could easily start another.

The dark night was illuminated only by the light from the flames. Dozens of men and women, some still in their nightclothes, had gathered to try to put out the fire. The barn was fully on fire when they arrived, and the roof of the house was smoking. Small licks of flame shot up in different places.

"Johnny, take a bucket and join the bucket brigade," his father directed him.

"Yes, sir," Johnny said. Thankfully for Ensign Williams, a town well was located directly across from his house, giving easy access to water. Johnny dropped his bucket at the well and, spying Nicholas in line, took a spot between him and Mrs. Hale.

Colonel Hale, Mr. Forsyth, Mrs. Keep, Miss Reynolds, Reverend Storrs, and even Margaret Pratt were there in the dark night. Several young men ran to the scene, bringing ladders from their own barns.

The Barn Fire

Turning to Nicholas, Johnny asked, "Did they get the animals out of the barn?"

"They did. I saw with my own eyes. They've been brought down to Colonel Hale's stable where they'll be safe."

"Good," said Johnny. "I was worried for them."

Captain Chapman had run to help some of the men who were quickly removing furniture and belongings from the house before the fire spread inside. They removed painted chests, chairs of all kids, a writing table, silver items, and a bass viol that had been used for a generation to play music during services. Someone came out carefully holding a stack of papers that he placed gingerly in the drawers of one of the dressers. Johnny even saw a pair of snowshoes and a pistol carried out. Anything and everything that could be removed from the house was taken out.

His classmates who lived in the house, Annie and Sam Williams, sat as still as stones in two of the armchairs that had been brought out onto the lawn. Their father worked frantically to direct the many helpers who had arrived. Poor Annie and Sam could do nothing but sit in the warm, damp night and watch their house slowly become engulfed in flames.

The rooster watched over it all, glowing in the light of the fire. As the sky slowly turned to shades of pink and orange in the east behind the house, it became clear how badly the fire had damaged the house and barn. As much as could have been saved was saved, but all that remained of the Williams house was a smoking pile of charred wood and the acrid smell of burnt timber. Lightning could be both beautiful and devastating—but today, on the town green, it was only devastating.

The townspeople of Longmeadow had come together and worked hard in the night, each knowing that there was always the chance that it could have been one of their homes that caught fire. They knew they would have received the same care. And when it was time to rebuild, they would be there for that as well.

Incorporation Day

A few days after the fire, the children returned to school. It was their last week to prepare for the Incorporation Day presentation, but it was so hard to concentrate on anything with the still-smoldering ruins of the Williams' house so nearby. The Widow Chandler invited the Williams family to stay with her until their house could be rebuilt. She said she had too many empty rooms, and they could stay for as long as they needed.

Annie and Sam Williams were back at school, grateful to have something to do besides feeling sad over what they had lost. Thankfully, the fire had burned slowly, and the townspeople had time to rescue so many family items. But still, they had lost their home. That left a gaping hole in their hearts and on the landscape of the town green.

The students of the brick schoolhouse were

putting the finishing touches on a poem they would be reciting at the big Incorporation Day celebration.

"Miss Reynolds, what does 'Incorporated' mean again?" asked Eda. "My family has lived here for over a hundred years. I don't understand how we are a new town!"

"Well," Miss Reynolds began, "I can see how that is confusing. You are right. There have been people living and working this land for many, many generations. Before your parents' ancestors came to this area, the people known as the Agawam were here. It's from the Agawam that Longmeadow got its name. They called this area 'Masacksic' which means 'the long meadow' in their language."

"I didn't know that!" said Johnny.

"Yes, it's the same for the river. We call it the Connecticut River, but the Agawam called it 'Kwinitekw,' which means 'long river.'"

All of the children quietly tried out the word "Kwinitekw," to see how it sounded and felt compared to how they knew it.

Miss Reynolds continued. "And you know what? The name Massachusetts even comes from the native people who were here when the English arrived. The Algonquin word 'Massadchu-es-et,' means 'great-hill-small-place,' possibly for the hills around Boston." The children all gave that word a try as well. "You *don't* need to be incorporated to be a community of people who live and work together, but you *do* need to be incorporated to be a town in the state of Massachusetts. Being incorporated means that Longmeadow will now get its name on the map of Massachusetts. And it is the first time a new town is being added to the map since the end of the war. That is quite an honor! Governor John Hancock himself is signing the proclamation. He was one of the signers of the Declaration of Independence a few years ago!"

The older students in the school had worked together to create an acrostic poem for the name LONGMEADOW. They would need to remember the poem and recite it to the whole town loudly and clearly.

"Ugh, I hate having to recite in front of the classroom. It's going to be even worse in front of the whole town!" Johnny said.

"I feel the same way," Nicholas said.

"I'm excited for it actually," Eda said. "Mother and Sylvie are working on something special for us to wear."

"Phillis is insisting on me having a new pair of shoes," Nicholas said.

"Well, I just have to hope I remember my shoes that day," Johnny groaned, making his friends laugh.

The school term flew by, and Johnny had grown so much as a student. He still wouldn't choose to spend his days inside if it were up to him, but the shame Master Loomis made him feel last term had been replaced by happier memories.

The morning of Incorporation Day dawned with rosy ribbons of pinks, violet, and orange light from the east. The air had a crispness that wasn't quite chilly but hinted that cooler days were coming. The town green was already bustling, and the ringing of the steeple bell called people to gather. Families packed picnic lunches and headed in. They came from the north end of the town near Springfield, the west by the river, the east where red sandstone was mined from rocky quarries, and the south where Enfield stood as the gateway to Connecticut.

A wooden stage had been built on the green for the day's speakers. The people had traded their work clothes for nice clothes. Men who had served in the war dressed in their uniform coats if they had one, and women and girls put on their freshest dresses and aprons. The young men and boys tucked their shirts neatly into their breeches and polished their shoes. Faces and hands were clean, and hair was tidy for the important day.

The Chapmans, including Johnny's two little brothers, had made it to the green. Little Nathaniel proudly followed Johnny around as he looked for Nicholas in the crowd. Eda and Hitty Keep found Johnny before Johnny found Nicholas. This often seemed to be the case.

"Johnny!" Eda cried. "There you are! Aw, is this your little brother? He's so cute! Look, Hitty! This is Johnny's little brother! Isn't he so cute?"

Hitty smiled and waved hello to

Nathaniel, happy to finally not be the youngest child for the moment.

"Yes, this is Nate. But have you seen Nicholas anywhere?"

"Yes, I saw him with Miss Phillis a little bit ago. But Miss Reynolds is here, too, and she's asked me to gather all the schoolchildren to meet for a quick rehearsal at the schoolhouse. You should hurry up and head there, too, and tell anyone else you see along the way."

Johnny quickly dropped Nathaniel back off with his parents—despite Nathaniel's protests—and headed to the schoolhouse. The poem had been living in his head for weeks. He'd recited it to his brothers, Mother Lucy, and just about every bird, squirrel, and chipmunk that would listen.

The brick schoolhouse was buzzing with excitement when Miss Reynolds called everyone to order. Nicholas was there, along with Willie and Lewis Cooley, Eda, Hitty, Margaret Pratt, Beulah Booth, and Annie and Samuel Williams, and all the other children who had attended the summer term of school. Out the windows, they could hear the high-pitched whistles of the fife players who had gathered under a nearby elm tree to rehearse.

Miss Reynolds quickly shut the door and windows to make it easier for everyone inside to listen and concentrate.

"All right, children, we don't have much time. Before we run through the poem one last time, I want to tell you how proud I am to stand with you today. I've treasured my time as your teacher, and I imagine that I've probably learned about as much from each of you as you've learned from me. Let's share this beautiful poem you've created together and make the people of Longmeadow proud."

The students quickly ran through their piece before joining their families in the crowd.

Soon, the speeches began. Upon the wooden stage sat all the important people who helped bring about the town's incorporation: Colonel Hale and Nathaniel Ely, John Bliss, and even the Governor of Massachusetts, John Hancock. Reverend Storrs was there to give the blessing.

Colonel Hale took the stage to welcome

everyone to the festivities.

"Long, indeed, and lovely is the meadow which stretches beside the quiet Connecticut River. Today is a special day in the history of our beloved community. Longmeadow now has the honor of being the first town incorporated in Massachusetts since the signing of the peace treaty with Great Britain, which made the nation and the state free and independent."
The crowd erupted with excited applause and cheers.

Governor Hancock stood to read the official proclamation: "Be it enacted by the Senate and House of Representatives in General Court that the Second Parish in Springfield called Longmeadow is hereby incorporated into a Town by the Name of Longmeadow, with all the powers and privileges that towns in this Commonwealth have and enjoy."

Another round of cheers erupted from the gathered crowd. Nathaniel, who was sitting on Johnny's lap in the grass, clapped along with everyone else, though he wasn't sure what he was clapping for. Nathaniel was just pleased to be part of the happy crowd.

As Governor Hancock continued reading the proclamation, Johnny scanned the crowd of familiar faces. Miss Phillis and Nicholas sat quietly in each other's company. Eda and Hitty Keep sat with their parents and older siblings, including Sylvie, who was still too focused on her upcoming wedding to be fun anymore. The green was filled to the brim with families who had called Longmeadow home for several generations already: the Blisses and Elys; the Cooleys and Burts; the Woolworths, Fields, and

Incorporation Day

Coltons. The Chapmans were there among them all on this day, and only time would tell if they, too, would stay for generations to come.

After the proclamation came a prayer from Reverend Storrs, music from the fife and drums, and a display from the militia. A picnic lunch was followed by the children's presentations. Johnny and his classmates gathered near the stage to await their turn. He stood with Nicholas, and it was easy to see that he, too, recited the words over and over to himself.

Finally, Miss Reynolds took the stage and motioned for her students to follow. Johnny had never seen the green from up on a stage, and especially not filled with so many faces watching him. Toward the middle of the crowd, Mother Lucy bounced Baby Abner on her knee, while his father held Nathaniel and pointed for him to wave to Johnny. Johnny gave a small wave back.

Miss Reynolds introduced them as the students of the brick schoolhouse's summer term who had composed their very own poem to commemorate the important day. And with that, it was time for the children to begin:

LONGMEADOW

L ovely town of green pastures and wide ways
    Where our school friends meet and we learn and play.

O verlooking the river once called "Kwinitekw"
    We admire its beauty and the fish that we've caught.

N ow here we meet on this beautiful day
    To stand and to share our thoughts in this way

G athered together on the pretty town green,
    We open our hearts on this day most serene.

M ay we always remember the lessons we've learned
    To work hard and be nice, our backs never turned.

E ach person has gifts to contribute for good,
    Sometimes in deeds and sometimes in words.

A dmit when you're wrong and avoid nasty looks,
    And learn to love numbers, your teacher, and books.

D elight in the bounty hard work always pays,
    Be grateful for families who love you all days.

O h! Happy we are for our dear little town,
    In sunshine, in snowtime, and when leaves fall down.

W hen years from now, wherever we roam,
    We'll always remember Longmeadow was home.

The crowd applauded, and one by one, each student took the quill pen in their hand and carefully signed the parchment on which the poem had been written. Older students signed for younger students who hadn't yet learned to write. Johnny signed last. And if he hadn't been so focused on not putting too much ink on the end of the quill, he would have realized that Phillis, Mother Lucy, and Captain Chapman all beamed proudly, knowing what an important accomplishment this was for him.

That night, after a dinner of fish, baked beans, green peas, and potato-apple pie, the family sat around the fire outside talking about the day.

"Well, Johnny, how does it feel to be an official signer of the 1783 Longmeadow School Poem?" his father teased.

Johnny laughed, "Good. My signature isn't perfect, but hopefully I'll have more chances to practice."

"Oh, I'm sure you will. You'll be signing deeds for land and business contracts before you know it. The country is growing so fast, and like I told Master Loomis all those months ago, it needs dreamers like you. You're a clever kid, Johnny. You'll go do great things."

"I go, too?" little Nathaniel asked.

"What's that, Nate?" Mother Lucy asked.

"I go, too? With Johnny? I go do great things, too?"

They all laughed.

"Well, now, not so fast, little one. I think you both have some more growing to do before you're ready to leave the nest," Mother Lucy said. "I need you both to be my little birds for a while longer before you fly out on your own. "

"Johnny, I go, too?" Nathaniel persisted, this time directing his question directly to his big brother.

"Don't worry, Nate. Wherever I go, you can come, too. Well…maybe not to school quite yet. It's hard to keep an eye on you and do my schoolwork. I don't think the brick schoolhouse is quite ready for you."

"OK, Johnny, but soon right? Soon I go with you?"

"Of course. We're a team," he said. And

with that, Nathaniel snuggled deep into his lap and yawned. Johnny stroked his little brother's curly hair and held him close in the warm glow of the firelight.

The still night surrounded them with the sounds of the crackling fire and crickets chirping. All was well in the Chapman's small little house in Longmeadow, Massachusetts.

School's Out

The week after Incorporation Day was the last week of school for the summer term. The time was spent tidying up the schoolroom and finishing assignments.

"Johnny, I don't know about you, but I'm looking forward to the end of this term," Nicholas said one morning as they waited outside for Miss Reynolds to ring the bell for the start of the day.

"I know," replied Johnny to his friend. "I mean, I've liked school so much better than I thought I would, but it's altogether too much sitting still for me. I didn't know how much I'd miss the fresh air and the trees until we got started!"

"And I didn't realize how much I like the time to pick and choose what I want to read and when I want to read it," Nicholas shared. "Don't get me wrong…I'm glad I came, and I've never seen Phillis so proud as when she was looking at my math copybook last night, but I am definitely ready for a break!"

A voice behind them surprised them. "Can I tell you boys a secret?"

It was Miss Reynolds. She appeared in the open window just above their heads. She had overheard their conversation. Leaning through the window, she whispered, "I'm ready for a break, too."

"You are?" Johnny asked, surprised.

"I sure am!" she responded with a hint of a smile. "Even teachers need breaks. As much as I've loved spending my days with you children, I'm missing my own family at home in Enfield. And my cats. I really miss my cats."

"You have cats?" Eda asked, appearing out of nowhere.

"I do! Three, actually. They spend a lot of time outside, but every evening they find their way back inside. My sister has been looking after them while I've been boarding with the Hales. I can't wait to have some time to sit with them on my lap purring and watching them chase sunbeams through the windows."

"Oh, I wish I could meet them," mused

Eda. "My mother says cats are only allowed inside if they are going to help keep mice out of the pantry. I would love a sweet little kitten to sleep curled up on my lap."

"We have a cat that visits the store every morning," added Nicholas. "Phillis lets me leave a little plate of cream out for it."

"Yes, I've seen him," said Miss Reynolds. "He never wants to let me pet him, though."

"We have some new kittens in our barn," said Johnny. "I'm sure you'd be welcome to come and visit them. Every morning before

Miss Reynolds' Cats

school, I bring my little brother out to check on them. I always make sure to keep a piece of string in my pocket for them to play with."

"You must have big pockets, Johnny!" Eda teased. "Pebbles and acorns and bird feathers and apple seeds and string. You always have something or other in there!"

"Johnny's got a good eye for what is useful and interesting, I think," said Miss Reynolds. "Now, who'd like to ring the bell for me this morning?"

Eda, of course, raised her hand first.

When school ended for the term, Johnny was free to spend his days at home again. Late summer was the beginning of a very busy time on family farms in New England. All times were busy on farms, but the change of seasons between the long, hot days of summer and the shorter, cooler days of fall were especially busy as farmers prepared to harvest the crops they had planted.

Captain Chapman was spending more time around the family's land and less time on carpentry and other odd jobs. He looked forward to having Johnny around again to help out.

Little Nathaniel was happiest of all though. Baby Abner wasn't nearly as fun as his big brother.

"Johnny, you staying home today?" he whispered into Johnny's face every morning as he woke him up in their shared trundle bed. And now, every day, Johnny could open one eye and look into his little brother's eager face and say yes.

Johnny's Mondays were back to fetching water from the brook for Mother Lucy's laundry day. He definitely felt a little lonely for his school friends. As he sat to take a break and have a snack between trips back and forth to Cooley Brook with his bucket, Mother Lucy asked him how he felt to be done.

"I'm not quite sure," Johnny answered. "I guess I'm happy to stretch my legs more and explore the woods, but I'm also a little sad that I can't share what I've found with Nicholas and Eda as easily. Now I have to set things aside and try to remember when I see them on the green. And since we only really head to the green for church on Sunday that's a lot of time to wait."

"I'm happy for you, Johnny," she said after a moment.

"You are?" he asked. "Happy that I can't see my friends?"

"Ha! No, of course not! I'm happy that you made such nice friends that you have someone to miss! I mean, remember back in the spring when Colonel Hale first gave you that delivery on the road and told you school was starting? Remember how frightened you were? You begged to stay home. But you went, and you liked it, and now you have so many new skills and memories and friends. That's why I'm happy for you, Johnny," she said, lean-

ing over to rumple the hair on his head. "In some ways, you look so much like your father, but there's a difference to you— a softness— that I bet you got from your mother. She'd be so proud of who you are becoming.

"Your father was a soldier and didn't hesitate to run towards battle. That's one kind of brave. But you are a whole other kind of brave. You are quietly brave. You had a fear and a shame that made you want to hide away at home…but you didn't. You went and faced the thing that made you scared. You didn't let one bad experience stop you from trying something again. And look at how you've grown. I'm so happy that my boys get to grow up with Johnny Chapman as their brother."

Johnny had never thought of himself as brave before. He sat taking in what his stepmother said. "Quietly brave," she had called him. If he had a pen and some paper, he'd have written that down. Instead, he just held onto it in his heart.

The Storrs House

Author's Note

Dear Reader,

    You may have noticed that this book opens with a short poem by Emily Dickinson. To me it perfectly sums up what my writing process for this book was like. The poem explores the idea that the creation of a vast and beautiful prairie of grass and flowers begins with two simple elements: one clover and a bee. And if you don't have those two ingredients, you can use "revery" - in other words… imagination! I used a combination of clover, bees AND "revery" to build Johnny Chapman's world. The clover and the bee for me were research about real people, places and events; the "revery" was my imaginings of what his daily life might have been like in the summer of 1783 in this small, New England community.

    Yes, Johnny Appleseed was a real person! His real last name was Chapman, not

Appleseed, and he was born in 1774 in Leominster, Massachusetts. Sadly, Johnny's mother died when he was only two years old and his father was away serving as a soldier in the Continental Army. Relatives in Leominster cared for Johnny and his older sister until his father remarried and settled in his new wife's hometown of Longmeadow, Massachusetts. Johnny was about seven years old and his sister probably stayed behind with the relatives in Leominster.

    Nearly every character in this book was absolutely a real person who lived in Longmeadow. Several of the events in the story were real, too - like the opening scene where Johnny receives a delivery of rum and sugar from Colonel Hale, and the fire at the Williams house on the green (though I did move that up in history to make Johnny Chapman a part of the action).

    I also drew inspiration from some of the famous myths about Johnny Appleseed as an adult, though it's important to remember that myths make great stories but they aren't always true (I mean, can you imagine anyone really wearing a tin pot as a hat?). I had a lot of fun playing with the ideas that Johnny loved nature and animals and that he never wore shoes!

Johnny Chapman lived in Longmeadow until at least 1791 when he was seventeen years old. Sometime in the mid-1790s, history finds him in western Pennsylvania, where he began collecting apple seeds from cider mills. He later headed farther west to Ohio, Illinois, and Indiana. He planted apple orchards so that families who were moving west like him could have things like cider to drink, potato-apple pie to eat, and cider vinegar to take the pain out of bee stings. The apples Johnny grew up with tasted different from the apples we know today, but they were as important a part of daily life then as they are today. Just as Mother Lucy said about the apple tree in their yard, "Even a house as small as ours can find room for a tree as useful as this."

The archives of the Longmeadow Historical Society have two records of Johnny Chapman's living here over a ten-year period.

The first is in Colonel Hale's account book, where he noted that Captain Nathaniel Chapman owed him money for rum and sugar "delivered [to] your boy." The second is a record of Johnny's seat assignment at the meetinghouse for church services, where he sat with the real-life Willie Cooley and Sam Williams, among others.

Longmeadow was Johnny Chapman's home for longer than he lived in any one place after that. Johnny's beautiful signature as "John Chapman" on several land deeds and promissory notes from his business dealings out west shows that he did indeed perfect his penmanship.

And, yes, history shows he really did take his little brother, Nathaniel, with him on his journey when he left.

If you'd like to learn more about the real history that inspired *Appleseeds: A Boy Named Johnny Chapman*, visit my website at www.appleseedsthebook.com.

Thanks for reading!
Melissa M. Cybulski
Longmeadow, Massachusetts

Acknowledgments

So many people have helped me bring *Appleseeds: A Boy Named Johnny Chapman* to life. First and foremost, I must thank Longmeadow resident, Diane Troderman, who made an appointment to hear about the work of the Longmeadow Historical Society. She insisted that children in town ought to know some of the great stories from our past. Her support, passion, and drive have kept this project moving forward and I'm grateful to know her.

Christina Cooper, children's librarian and author, shared her "can do" attitude from the beginning! I am so grateful to her for everything from teaching me the basics of word count and line spacing to looking at my earliest pages and encouraging me to join the SCBWI.

None of this would have been possible without my friends in the history community.

There was no question Dennis Picard couldn't answer - whether it be about digging wells or the (in)authenticity of people cheering "Huzza!" Elizabeth and David Marinelli shared their expertise on a walk around Laurel Park about the types of plants and trees that Johnny would have known as a child. Tom Kelleher of Old Sturbridge Village indulged me with an interview about apple trees, orchards, and cider mills in early New England. Old Sturbridge Village is the best place to go to really immerse yourself in the sensory world of early Massachusetts!

Dr. William Kerrigan, of Muskingum University in Ohio, talked with me about his experience jogging around Longmeadow to get a sense of the space Johnny grew up in as research for his fantastic book, *Johnny Appleseed and the American Orchard*. He's one of the few Johnny Appleseed scholars who truly spent time trying to piece together a view of post-war Longmeadow and the Cooley family that Captain Chapman married into. Mary Marotta, of the Leominster Historical Society, was my personal tour guide of the birthplace of Johnny

Chapman, driving me around to show me key landmarks.

My colleagues Al McKee, Betsy McKee, and Beth Hoff of the Longmeadow Historical Society deserve a special thank you for always being willing to "play" with me as I made my way through the archival resources at the Storrs House Museum. Their professionalism and dedication to preserving and sharing the history of this little town with big stories is an inspiration.

The children and 3rd-grade teachers at Center, Wolf Swamp, and Blueberry Hill schools in Longmeadow welcomed me in for local history lessons and reminded me how much fun it is to share history with a roomful of eager young minds! I am particularly indebted to Teddy Steger and his family. Teddy earnestly approached me after a classroom visit and asked if he could read my book when it was done. He and his family read the first draft from a three-ring binder and offered such helpful and encouraging feedback.

The children's librarians in the Discovery Room at the Richard Salter Storrs Library were a great support and helped me gather the kids for our *Tuesdays with Johnny Appleseed* group. Thank you for braving the quill pens and inkwells alongside me!

T. Lak, illustrator and graphic designer, brought life to my pages in wonderful ways.

And last, but always first, my family. Thank you to my parents, Joy and Matthew McCrosson, whose pride and confidence in me encourage me to believe I can do anything. My husband, Mark, shines as an eagle-eyed editor and always reminds me that it's okay to take the time and space I need to lose myself in my projects. And my children, Millie and Ben, who let me read wonderful books to them at bedtime for so many years, have filled my head with stories and my heart with love.

Melissa M. Cybulski

Melissa M. Cybulski lives in Western Massachusetts with her husband, two children, and two pugs. She loves learning and writing about history, especially the lives of women and children in early New England. Even as a child, historical fiction and biographies of people who lived long ago lined the bookcase in her room. This book about Johnny Chapman, who would one day be known as Johnny Appleseed, grew out of her work with the Longmeadow Historical Society. When not researching and writing, she works as a guide at the Emily Dickinson Museum in Amherst, Massachusetts.

T.Lak

T. Lak has been an award winning illustrator for over 55 years. This is his 5th book on amazon, his 4th children's book. His concepts and designs have been seen world-wide with his work at a Fortune 100 financial company. His clients included MassMutual Financial Group, Bradley International Airport, Professional Drywall Company; Polish Center of Discovery and Learning as well as many others. His resume includes work created for videos, multi media, logos and billboards. In his career, his caricatures have adorned hundreds of walls.

Made in the USA
Middletown, DE
23 May 2024

54527868R00097